A Short Guide to English Composition

William A. McQueen
University of North Carolina

Third Edition

Wadsworth Publishing Company
A Division of Wadsworth, Inc.
Belmont, California

Designer: Rick Chafian Cover Designer: Detta Penna

Production Editor: Sandra Craig

Printed in the United States of America
1 2 3 4 5 6 7 8 9 10—83 82 81 80 79

Library of Congress Cataloging in Publication Data

McQueen, William A
A short guide to English composition.

Includes index.
1. English language—Rhetoric. 2. English language—Grammar—1950– I. Title.
PE1408.M3324 1979 808′.042 78-24550
ISBN 0–534–00703–1

Acknowledgments

The American Historical Association, for the paragraph from Carl Becker, "Everyman His Own Historian," *The American Historical Review,* January 1932.

Collins-Knowlton-Wing, Inc., for the paragraph from Suetonius, *Twelve Caesars,* translated by Robert Graves. Penguin L72, Baltimore 1957. Copyright 1957 by International Authors N. V.

Doubleday & Company, Inc., for the paragraph from Edward T. Hall, *The Silent Language,* a Premier Book, New York, 1961.

Farrar, Straus & Giroux, Inc., for the selection from Joan Didion, *Slouching towards Bethlehem.* Copyright © 1966, 1968 by Joan Didion. Reprinted by permission of Farrar, Straus & Giroux, Inc.

Northrup Frye, for the passage on leisure from his 1958 university lecture.

John Gardner, for the excerpts from his book *The Resurrection.* Copyright © 1966 by John Gardner. Reprinted by permission of the author.

The Green Caldron, a publication of freshman themes at the University of Illinois, for paragraphs from student themes and several illustrated examples from its "Rhet as Writ" section.

Harcourt Brace Jovanovich, Inc., for one sentence from Lewis Mumford, *The Culture of Cities,* 1970.

Harper & Row, Publishers, Inc., for the paragraph from O. C. Rölvaag, *Giants in the Earth,* 1927, and for the paragraph from John F. Kennedy, *The Burden and the Glory,* edited by Allan Nevins, 1964.

Harvard University, for the paragraph from Walter Lippmann, "The Nuclear Age," *Atlantic,* May 1962. Copyright © 1962 by The Atlantic Monthly Company, Boston, Mass. Reprinted by permission of the President and Fellows of Harvard College.

William Morrow and Company, Inc., for the paragraph from Joseph Wood Krutch, *The Twelve Seasons.* New York: Apollo Editions, Inc. Copyright 1949 by Joseph Wood Krutch.

Louis A. Muinzer, for the paragraphs from "History: The Life in Language," *Illinois English Bulletin,* May 1960.

Prentice-Hall, Inc., for the paragraphs from Ina Corinne Brown, *Understanding Other Cultures,* © 1963. Reprinted by permission of Prentice-Hall, Inc., Englewood Cliffs, N.J.

University of North Carolina, for the paragraph from Van Hartmann, "The Silents: From Melies to Keaton," in *An Introduction to Film Criticism,* edited by Jeffrey H. Richards. Chapel Hill, N.C.: Department of English, University of North Carolina, 1977.

Contents

For the summer builders:

Ida Glynn, Anne, Ellen, Ashley, and Chester

Preface to the Third Edition

In response to the suggestions of a number of readers, I have expanded some parts of this book. It is still, however, a little book whose aim is to provide clear and simple explanations of specific writing problems. It offers, through the keys inside the front and back covers, quick access to the kind of information that a student needs while writing or revising a paper.

The book can easily be used as a theme correction guide. The instructor simply underlines an error and puts the appropriate sign in the margin. The ease of access and the conciseness of the entries should allow the student to identify the nature of his or her error and make the correction with a minimum of difficulty. Of course, the student can also use the book to avoid errors. Like a dictionary, it is a reference tool and should be used often.

Since it does not have a dominating structure and since it deals with the essentials of English usage, *A Short Guide* can blend easily and inconspicuously with a variety of books and rhetorical approaches.

The following changes have been made for the third edition:

Grammar

Section G 1, Adjective and Adverb Forms, has been revised and expanded. Section G 3, Agreement of Subject and Verb, has been greatly expanded; it now contains eleven subsections, with fuller explanations and many new examples. The comment on Mood has been slightly expanded and moved from the List of Terms to section G 5. New sections on Tense (G 7) and Voice (G 8) have been added.

Sentence Structure

This chapter has been greatly expanded. An entirely new part, Building Sentences, has been inserted at the beginning. Much of the Common Problems in Sentences segment is unchanged, but fairly extensive revisions have been made in sections S 4, Parallelism; S 5, Coordination; and S 6, Subordination. Section S 10, Confusing Elliptical Clauses, and section S 15, Sentence Variety, have been slightly expanded, and a new section (S 8) has been added on Mixed Constructions. Also, exercises in sentence building and further suggestions have been added under the heading Improving Your Skills.

Clarity of Thought

Only minor changes have been made except for the additions to section C 6, Transition, and to section C 7, Vague Generality.

Diction

Three new sections have been added: Idiomatic Usage (D 6), Connotation (D 8), and Varieties of Usage (D 9). Also, new entries have been added to the Word Choice section (D 10).

Punctuation

A new subsection has been added to section Pu 4, Comma; a new section has been added on Creative Punctuation (Pu 23); and a few minor changes have been made in other sections.

Mechanics

Section M 5, Numbers, has been revised. The section on documentation has been divided into two sections: Footnotes and

Endnotes (M 3) and Bibliography (M 4). These sections have also been revised to bring them more into accord with the new *MLA Handbook* and have been expanded with examples of the citation of nonprinted media.

Spelling

This chapter has been reorganized. The spelling rules now come first. Suggestions for correcting misspelled words and a list of frequently misspelled words have been included under the heading Improving Your Skills.

Paragraphs

The subsection on Coherence (Pa 1.2) has been slightly expanded; a new example of development by definition has been provided (Pa 2.7); and a new subsection has been added on Classification and Division (Pa 2.9).

From Beginning to End: The Whole Paper

This entirely new chapter includes sections on Prewriting and Revising.

A List of Terms

A few entries have been omitted or revised, and new entries have been added.

Theme Topics

Some topics have been dropped, and more than two hundred new topics have been added.

In this new edition, as in the previous editions, I want to thank all of those who have contributed to the making of this book, especially Bob Bain, Jo Gibson, and Nannette Mengel; the reviewers: John Clifford, Queens College; Tom Hemmens, Kansas State University; Eric Hibbison, J. Sargeant Reynolds Community College; Patricia Licklider, John Jay College; Homer Lusk, Grossmont College; Peter T. Zoller, Wichita State University; and Randy Cade and Sandra Craig.

William A. McQueen

Grammar

G 1 ADJECTIVE AND ADVERB FORMS

Adjectives and adverbs have two degrees of comparison: **comparative** and **superlative.**

The **comparative degree** expresses a greater or lesser degree of comparison.

The **superlative degree** expresses the greatest or lowest degree of comparison.

POSITIVE COMPARISONS

	Word	*Comparative*	*Superlative*
Adjectives	cold	colder	coldest
	easy	easier	easiest
	active	more active	most active
	healthy	healthier	healthiest
		or	*or*
		more healthy	most healthy
	beautiful	more beautiful	most beautiful
Adverbs	coldly	more coldly	most coldly
	easily	more easily	most easily
	actively	more actively	most actively

Adjectives of one syllable use the suffixes *-er* and *-est* to form the comparative and the superlative (*colder, coldest*). Some adjectives of two syllables use *-er, -est* (*easier, easiest*), whereas others use *more, most* (*more active, most active*); some adjectives of two syllables use either form (*healthier, healthiest* or *more healthy, most healthy*). Adjectives of more than two syllables use *more, most* rather than *-er, -est* (*more beautiful, most beautiful*). With a few rare exceptions, adverbs use the forms *more, most* rather than *-er, -est* (*more easily, most easily*).

NEGATIVE COMPARISONS

	Word	*Comparative*	*Superlative*
Adjectives	cold	less cold	least cold*
	easy	less easy	least easy*
	active	less active	least active
Adverbs	coldly	less coldly	least coldly
	easily	less easily	least easily
	actively	less actively	least actively

*Sometimes the thought can be expressed more effectively by using another word positively rather than using a negative comparison: e.g., *warmer* rather than *less cold, hottest* rather than *least cold,* or *hardest* rather than *least easy.* As you may have noticed, some of the superlative forms are rarely used.

Some words—for instance, *good* (*better, best*), *bad* (*worse, worst*), *well* (*better, best*)—compare irregularly; and some words—*dead, unique,* and *empty*—cannot logically have superlative forms. Sometimes, however, an illogical comparison can produce a vivid phrase, such as "deader than a doornail" (a cliché now) or "the emptiest head in Chatham County."

Special Problems

1. The comparative form of adjectives is used in a comparison of two things; the superlative is used in a comparison of more than two.

COMPARATIVE

John is *faster* than Frank.

May the *better* team win.
(referring to two)

SUPERLATIVE

John is the *fastest* man on the team.

May the *best* team win.
(referring to more than two)

Also see *worse* in D 10.

2. The comparative forms of adjectives and adverbs are often confused. Do not use an adjective form where an adverbial form is needed.

My roommate reads Spanish *more easily* (not *easier*) than I do.
(Since an adverb is needed to modify the verb *reads*, the adverbial form *more easily* is used instead of the adjective form *easier*. You would not, for example, say "My roommate reads Spanish easy," but "My roommate reads Spanish *easily*.")

Hemingway wrote *more simply* (not *simpler*) than Faulkner.

Connors played *more fiercely* (not *fiercer*) than his opponent.

Also see *good* and *bad* in D 10.

G 2 AGREEMENT OF PRONOUN AND ANTECEDENT

A pronoun agrees with its antecedent in person and number and sometimes in gender.

Everyone in the room focused *his* attention on Jim.

Sara and *Jane* focused *their* attention on Jim.

Jane nodded *her* approval.

John nodded *his* approval.

Have *you* found *your* keys?

Special Problem

Since indefinite pronouns such as *anyone, somebody, each, either* are singular, pronouns referring to them should be singular in form as in the first example above.

This usage is complicated by the fact that some people object to the use of the inclusive masculine form *his* to refer to both sexes; but *her* is no more satisfactory, and the solution of using both masculine and feminine forms is rather unwieldy. One might be inclined to abandon the traditional insistence on the use of a singular pronoun in such instances and to simply use *their,* as many people do in their conversation. But if this practice is followed as a general principle, it can lead to other agreement problems. Consider this sentence:

Everyone *thinks* that *their* way is best.

Everyone cannot be both singular and plural, yet in this sentence it agrees with a singular verb (*thinks,* instead of *think*) and with a plural pronoun (*their*). Until this problem is resolved by usage, the most practical solution for anyone who objects to the use of the masculine form to refer to both sexes seems to be to use the double reference, *his* or *her.*

G 3 AGREEMENT OF SUBJECT AND VERB

A verb agrees with its subject in person and number.

Problems of subject-verb agreement occur because of variations in the verb forms for first, second, and third person in some tenses, as in the third person singular of the present and present perfect tenses of most verbs or, somewhat more extensively, in the verb *be*.

	Singular	*Plural*
	Present tense of *know*	
First person	I know	We know
Second person	You know	You know
Third person	He, she, it *knows**	They know
	Present perfect tense of *know*	
First person	I have known	We have known
Second person	You have known	You have known
Third person	He, she, it *has* known	They have known
	Present tense of *be*	
First person	I *am*	We are
Second person	You are	You are
Third person	He, she, it *is*	They are
	Past tense of *be*	
First person	I *was*	We were
Second person	You were	You were
Third person	He, she, it *was*	They were
	Present perfect tense of *be*	
First person	I have been	We have been
Second person	You have been	You have been
Third person	He, she, it *has* been	They have been

*In contrast to nouns, which add an *s* in the plural form, verbs add an *s* in the *singular*.

Actually, there are further inflectional variations in the verb *be* and in the passive versions of *know,* but these examples should serve our purpose here.

If there is any difficulty in subject-verb agreement, it usually involves (1) identifying the subject (i.e., the specific word with which the verb should agree) and determining whether it is singular or plural, or (2) knowing what to do when the verb has more than one subject.

The constructions and the kinds of words that are likely to cause problems are listed below.

1. *And* constructions. Two or more subjects joined by *and* require a plural verb, even if each subject is singular.

> *John and Mary were* late for class.

2. *Or, nor* constructions. When two or more subjects are joined by *or* or *nor,* the verb is singular if both of the subjects are singular. If one of the subjects is singular and the other is plural, the verb agrees with the one nearer to it.

> Either *love or hate is* preferable to indifference.
> (Since both subjects are singular, the verb is singular.)
>
> Either the referee or the *players were* mistaken.
>
> Either the players or the *referee was* mistaken.
> (In these sentences the verb agrees with the subject nearer to it.)

A third possibility would be to rephrase the sentence so that the agreement problem is avoided:

> *Someone was mistaken,* either the players or the referee.
>
> Either the *players were* mistaken, or the *referee was.*

3. Intervening phrases. Do not be misled by phrases which intervene between the subject and the verb.

Each of the players *was* introduced.
(The subject is *each,* not *players*.)

The *coach,* as well as the players, *was* elated by the victory.
(Although the phrase *as well as* has an effect similar to *and,* it introduces a subordinate addition as a kind of afterthought rather than the second part of a compound subject. The intervening phrase does not influence the agreement between the subject and the verb. The sentence could, of course, be written, "The coach and the players were elated by the victory," but that would be a different sentence.)

The *defendant,* with his lawyers, *was* watching the witness intently.
(The subject is *defendant.* The phrase *with his lawyers* has no effect upon the number of the verb.)

4. Subjects and predicate nouns. When a clause contains a predicate noun, the verb agrees with the subject, not with the predicate noun.

My main *interest is* boats.

Boats are my main interest.

5. *There is, there are* constructions. In *there is* or *there are* constructions, the subject follows the verb and determines its number.

There *are* many *answers* to that question.

There *is* only one *solution*.

This rule also applies when a compound subject follows the verb.

In the front room there *are* only a *chair,* a *desk,* and a *wastebasket*.

(The problem could be avoided in this case by rephrasing the sentence: "The front *room contains* only a chair, desk, and a wastebasket.")

6. Clauses with relative pronouns as subjects. In constructions such as the following, the relative pronoun *who* is usually plural, in agreement with the nearest possible antecedent, and requires a plural verb.

John is one of those *students who are* always prepared.

He is one of those *athletes who play* best under pressure.

7. Constructions such as *most of, some of*. *Most of, some of, all of,* and fractions such as *two-thirds of* may be either singular or plural, depending upon whether the word after the preposition is singular or plural.

Most (some, all, two-thirds) of the students *were* present.

Most (some, all, two-thirds) of the cake *was* left.

A number of and *none of* may be either singular or plural even though the word after the preposition is plural.

A number of wrecks *have* occurred at that intersection.
(meaning *many*)

A number of wrecks *has* occurred at that intersection.
(with emphasis on the idea of a number)

None of the students *were* present.
(meaning *not any*)

None of the students *was* present.
(meaning *not one*)

8. Collective nouns. Collective nouns, such as *class, team, audience, family, committee, jury, couple, crowd,* are considered to be singular when thought of as a collective unit.

The *team respects* Coach Smith.

The *audience was* restless.

When the emphasis is on the individual members which comprise the unit, a plural verb can sometimes be used, but if the construction seems awkward, the best procedure is to rephrase the sentence.

The *players respect* Coach Smith.

The *members* of the audience *were* restless.

The most troublesome problems with collective nouns occur when there is a question of both verb agreement and pronoun agreement in the same sentence. The main thing to remember in such a situation is not to make the collective noun both singular and plural in the same sentence. Do not, for instance, say, ''The couple *has* (singular verb) spoiled *their* (plural noun) only child.'' You could make both the verb and the pronoun singular or you could make them both plural, but since both of these versions would be somewhat awkward, the best solution seems to be to rephrase the sentence.

Tom and Joan have spoiled their only child.

9. Words ending in *-ist*. Sometimes what seems to be an agreement error is actually a spelling problem, particularly in words ending in *-ist*. Since words like *scientist, dentist, artist* have similar sounds in the singular (*scientist*) and in the plural (*scientists*), some people forget to add an *s* when they are referring to more than one.

INCORRECT

Scientist work in laboratories, and *artist* work in studios.

CORRECT

Scientists work in laboratories, and *artists* work in studios.

10. Words that are always plural. Words like *pants, scissors, pliers, glasses, jeans* are always plural.

> Mondale's pants *were* short.
>
> My glasses *are* broken.
>
> Jeans *are* becoming popular throughout the world.

11. Words ending in *-ics*. Generally, words ending in *-ics* are singular when they refer to branches of science and plural when they refer to activities or qualities.

> Mathematics *is* my most difficult subject.
>
> Economics *is* not yet an exact science.
>
> *but*
>
> The acoustics in the new auditorium *are* excellent.
>
> Athletics *are* an important part of collegiate life.

When in doubt concerning words ending in *-ics,* consult your dictionary.

G 4 CASE OF NOUNS AND PRONOUNS

Although English once had a complex system of case inflections, only three cases (nominative, possessive, and objective) are in use today, and inflectional changes have decreased even in these three cases. At one time a noun would be spelled one way if it were the subject of a sentence (nominative case) and another way if it were the direct object (objective case), but now the language is more dependent on word order than on spelling changes to indicate how a word is used in a sentence. All nouns and many pronouns are spelled alike in the nominative and objective cases (*John, John*), changing in spelling only to indicate the possessive case (*John's*), but the personal pronouns *I, he, she, we, they,* and the relative pronoun *who* have different forms for each case.

Nominative	I	he	she	we	they	who
Possessive	my (mine)	his	her (hers)	our (ours)	their (theirs)	whose
Objective	me	him	her	us	them	whom

1. Nominative case (*I, he, she, we, they, who*). Subjects and predicate nouns are in the nominative case.

SUBJECT

Who is John?

He knows John.

PREDICATE NOUN

Who is *he?*

Do not be misled by constructions in which a whole clause is the object of a preposition or verb.

Give the book to *whoever* asks for it.
(*Whoever* is the subject of the verb *asks,* and the whole clause, *whoever asks for it,* is the object of the preposition *to.*)

Choose *whoever* is best qualified for the job.
(*Whoever* is the subject of the verb *is,* and the whole clause, *whoever is best qualified for the job,* is the object of the verb *choose.*)

Do not be misled by intervening phrases such as *I think* or *you believe.*

Who do you think will win?
(*Who* is the subject of the verb *will win,* not the object of the verb *do think.*)

2. Objective case (*me, him, her, us, them, whom*). The following are in the objective case:

DIRECT OBJECTS

I like *her*.

INDIRECT OBJECTS

She gave *me* the key.

OBJECTS OF PREPOSITIONS

Just between you and *me* . . .

Frank sent the letter to *her* and *Jimmy*.

OBJECTS OF VERBALS

Seeing *him* was quite a surprise.

I was glad to see *him*.

SUBJECTS OF INFINITIVES

I asked *him* to go with us.

3. Possessive case (*my, his, her, its, our, their, whose*). Instead of indicating the function of a word in the structure of a sentence, the possessive case indicates a relationship between two nouns, a noun and a gerund, or a pronoun and a following noun or gerund.

John's car

her typing

a *day's* work

John's family objects to *his* (not *him*) drinking.

We all admire *Frank's* singing.

The possessive of nouns is formed in the following ways:

(a) *for all words that do not end in* s: add an apostrophe and an *s*.

boy ⟶ boy's

man ⟶ man's

men ⟶ men's

children ⟶ children's

(b) *for plural nouns that end in* s: add an apostrophe only.

boys ⟶ boys'

bosses ⟶ bosses'

(c) *for singular nouns that end in* s: add an apostrophe and an *s* if you pronounce the additional *s;* if you do not, add an apostrophe only.

boss ⟶ boss's

Jones ⟶ Jones's or Jones'

Williams ⟶ Williams's or Williams'

(d) *for coordinate nouns in the possessive case:* add the apostrophe or the apostrophe and *s* only after the last noun.

The party is going to be at John and Mary's house.

Note: An apostrophe is not used in the possessive form of personal or relative pronouns.

his, hers, its, ours, theirs, whose

Special Problems

1. Appositive pronouns. Appositive pronouns are in the same case as words with which they are in apposition.

We—John and *I*—left to get the car.

She gave the cake to us—John and *me*.

We boys left early.

She gave the cake to *us* boys.

Note: In the last two examples the case would be easier to determine if you imagined the sentence without the appositive nouns (*boys*). You would not say *us left,* or *to we*.

2. Pronouns in elliptical clauses. In elliptical clauses the case of a pronoun is determined by what its function would be in the clause if the thought of the clause were completely stated.

He is taller than *I* (am tall).

She likes Henry better than (she likes) *me*.

She likes Henry better than *I* (like Henry).

3. Pronouns in pairs. Do not assume that all pronouns in pairs are in the nominative case. The case of the pronouns is determined by the function of the pronouns in the sentence, not by the fact that they are in pairs.

NOMINATIVE

He and *I* are going to Europe this summer.
(He and *I* are subjects of the verb.)

OBJECTIVE

Carol smiled at *him* and *me*.
(*Him* and *me* are the objects of the preposition.)

G 5 MOOD

There are three moods in English: *indicative, imperative,* and *subjunctive*. Of these three, the indicative is by far the most common. It is, in fact, the norm from which the other two vary. The indicative mood is the form of expository, factual statement.

I am hungry.

The imperative mood indicates a command or strong request. It is easily recognized by the fact that it characteristically omits the subject, which is understood but not written.

Be quiet.

Close the door.

The subjunctive mood indicates a wish, doubt, requirement, possibility, concession, or condition contrary to fact. The subjunctive inflections are rapidly disappearing from the language, and the subjunctive function is being increasingly assumed by auxiliaries such as *may, might, could, should, ought to*. Subjunctive inflections survive mainly in *if* and *that* clauses expressing conditions contrary to fact or required action and in idioms such as *God help us, suffice it to say, if need be*.

If I *were* (instead of *was*) rich.

God *forbid* (instead of *forbids*).

I move that the meeting *be* adjourned (instead of *is* adjourned).

The constitution requires that a candidate for the U.S. Senate *be* (instead of *is*) at least thirty years old.

We *may be* (instead of *are*) able to attend the concert.

G 6 REFERENCE OF PRONOUNS

Vague or ambiguous pronoun reference often causes misunderstanding. The following problems, in particular, are likely to cause trouble. Be alert for them, and try to avoid them.

1. Ambiguous reference of a pronoun to its antecedent. A pronoun should refer to its antecedent clearly.

AMBIGUOUS

When Smith first met Jones, he had a beard.
(The pronoun *he* is ambiguous. It might refer to Smith or to Jones. The reference is not clear.)

CLEAR

Smith had a beard when he first met Jones.

When Smith first met him, Jones had a beard.

2. Awkward separation of a pronoun from its antecedent. Place pronouns as near to their antecedents as possible. If pronouns are separated from their antecedents by intervening words or phrases, they may seem to modify the wrong word.

MISPLACED

He stood by the *car* as the afternoon sun beat mercilessly upon the asphalt *which* he had just polished.

CLEARER

As the afternoon sun beat mercilessly upon the asphalt, he stood by the *car which* he had just polished.

3. Reference of a pronoun to a subordinate construction. Avoid having a pronoun refer to a subordinate construction which is not in the forefront of the reader's mind as he scans the sentence.

CONFUSING

The morning mail was placed on Professor Macmillan's desk. It was made of sturdy oak.
(At first glance the reader tends to assume that *it* refers to *mail.* The sentence is momentarily confusing.)

CLEARER

The morning mail was placed on Professor Macmillan's sturdy oak desk.

4. Reference of a pronoun to an implied antecedent. Do not use a pronoun to refer to an antecedent which is implicit but not actually stated. Such references are frequently awkward or confusing.

VAGUE REFERENCE

Although many of his friends are fishermen, he does not enjoy *it*.
(There is no antecedent to which the pronoun *it* can logically refer.)

CLEAR

Although many of his friends enjoy *fishing*, he does not care for *it*.
(*Fishing* is clearly the antecedent of *it*.)

5. Indefinite reference of *which, this, they, you,* or *it*. Some writers habitually use the pronouns *which, this, they, you,* and *it* to refer to vague or indefinite antecedents. Sometimes the meaning may be perfectly clear, but the frequent use of such reference will sooner or later cause confusion. As a general rule, either have these pronouns refer to specific antecedents or rephrase the sentence so that a pronoun is not necessary.

VAGUE REFERENCE

Fitzgerald was disguised in a large black mustache, *which* I recognized at once.
(Although *which* was intended to refer to the whole preceding clause, it seems to refer to *mustache*.)

CLEAR

I recognized Fitzgerald at once, although he was wearing a large black mustache.

VAGUE REFERENCE

Although the early returns favored his opponent, Smith remained calm. He had learned *this* from long experience.

REPHRASED

Smith eyed his opponent's lead without emotion. He had learned from long experience to remain calm during the early returns.

VAGUE REFERENCE

They show too many commercials on television.

BETTER

Too much television time is allotted to commercials.

AWKWARD REFERENCE

In the newspaper *it* says that we shall have rain tomorrow.

BETTER

The newspaper predicts rain for tomorrow.

G 7 TENSE

The Six Tenses

There are six tenses in English: the **present, past, future, present perfect, past perfect,** and **future perfect**.

All of these tenses are formed from the three principal parts of verbs. The first principal part of a verb is the normal form of the verb as it is listed in the dictionary—for instance, *see*. The second principal part is the past form (*saw*). The third principal part is the past participle (*seen*).

Each tense has different forms for the active and passive voice.

In the **active voice,** the present and the future tenses are based on the first principal part, the past tense is based on the second principal part, and the three perfect tenses are based on the third principal part in combination with the appropriate tenses of the verb *have*.

In the **passive voice,** all six tenses are based on the third principal part in combination with the appropriate tenses of the verb *be*.

As an example of tense formation, the verb *see* is given below in all six tenses in both the active and the passive voices (indicative mood). The principal parts are *see, saw, seen*.

Active Voice		*Passive Voice*	
	Present Tense		
I see	We see	I am seen	We are seen
You see	You see	You are seen	You are seen
He }	They see	He }	They are seen
She } sees		She } is seen	
It }		It }	
	Past Tense		
I saw	We saw	I was seen	We were seen
You saw	You saw	You were seen	You were seen
He }	They saw	He }	They were seen
She } saw		She } was seen	
It }		It }	

Active Voice		*Passive Voice*	
	Future Tense		
I will* see	We will* see	I will* be seen	We will* be seen
You will see	You will see	You will be seen	You will be seen
He / She / It } will see	They will see	He / She / It } will be seen	They will be seen
	Present Perfect Tense		
I have seen	We have seen	I have been seen	We have been seen
You have seen	You have seen	You have been seen	You have been seen
He / She / It } has seen	They have seen	He / She / It } has been seen	They have been seen
	Past Perfect Tense		
I had seen	We had seen	I had been seen	We had been seen
You had seen	You had seen	You had been seen	You had been seen
He / She / It } had seen	They had seen	He / She / It } had been seen	They had been seen
	Future Perfect Tense		
I will* have seen	We will* have seen	I will* have been seen	We will* have been seen
You will have seen	You will have seen	You will have been seen	You will have been seen

Active Voice		Passive Voice	
He / She / It will have seen	They will have seen	He / She / It will have been seen	They will have been seen

*Either *shall* or *will* may be used in the first person of the future and future perfect tenses, *shall* being more formal. Only *will* is used for the second and third person forms of these tenses.

Verbs such as *see* are called **irregular verbs** because all of the principal parts are different. Verbs such as *walk (walked, walked)* and *dream (dreamed, dreamed),* which have the same form for the second and third principal parts, are called **regular verbs**. The principal parts of irregular verbs are listed after the verb in any good dictionary. The principal parts of regular verbs (which simply add *-ed* to the verb) are not usually given in dictionary entries.

The **present tense** indicates present time, a general truth, or a habitual action.

It *is* cold today.

February *is* a cold month.

We *play* chess every evening.

The **past tense** indicates a time before the moment of speaking or writing.

It *was* cold yesterday.

The **future tense** indicates a time after the moment of speaking or writing.

It *will be* cold tomorrow.

The **present perfect** tense indicates a general rather than a precisely limited moment in the past, frequently with the implication of a continuing action.

Compare, for instance, the verbs in the following sentences:

PAST

I *lost* my watch.

PRESENT PERFECT

I *have lost* my watch.

PAST

He *was* happy.

PRESENT PERFECT

He *has been* happy.

Notice that you could say "I lost my watch Tuesday night," or "He was happy Tuesday night," but not "I have lost my watch Tuesday night" or "He has been happy Tuesday night." The past tense can easily refer to a particular moment in the past. The present perfect tense refers to the past in a more general way.

The **past perfect** tense refers to a moment in the past prior to another moment in the past.

I suddenly *realized* that I *had lost* my watch.
(The first verb, *realized,* is in the simple past tense. The second verb, *had lost,* which refers to a time prior to the time of the first verb, is in the past perfect tense.)

The **future perfect** tense refers to a moment in the future prior to another moment in the future. The action occurs *after* the present but *before* another time in the future.

By this time next Tuesday, she *will have arrived* in Paris.
(The verb, *will have arrived,* is in the future perfect tense. It refers to a time in the future which is prior to another future time, *next Tuesday*.)

Auxiliaries

Auxiliary verbs are verbs which combine with other verbs to form variations in tense, voice, or mood. The principal auxiliary verbs are *be, can, do, have, may, shall,* and *will.*

For examples of *be, have,* and *will* used as auxiliary verbs see the conjugation of the verb *see* on pages 19–21.

Be and *have* can be inflected through all of the six tenses, but *can, do, may, shall,* and *will* have only two forms.

can	could
do	did
may	might
shall	should
will	would

These forms can be used to show differences in time, but they do not always do so. Sometimes they are used to indicate mood rather than tense. Often they do both simultaneously.

An old rule that is no longer consistently followed said that *shall* should be used for the first person of the future and future perfect tenses and that *will* should be used for the second and third persons.

	Future Tense	
First person	I shall see	We shall see
Second person	You will see	You will see
Third person	He will see	They will see

Increasingly, however, *will* is being used for first person as well as for second and third persons.

On the other hand, the rule stated that *will* should be used in the first person and *shall* in the second and third person to express resolution or determination rather than tense.

This rule had the advantage of providing a formula for distinguishing between the use of *shall* and *will* to signify tense and their use to signify mood, but the rule simply has not been adhered to with any consistency in American usage. You would not be wrong if you followed it in formal writing, but in less formal contexts *shall* strikes some readers as being stilted, and it is being used less now than it was formerly.

The forms *should* and *would* are increasingly being used to signify mood.

I *should* study harder.
(To the extent that *should* signifies time at all, it suggests a future action. Its primary function is to express an attitude of obligation toward the act of studying. In other words, it indicates the mood of the verb.)

She *should* win.
(Here *should* is used primarily to indicate probability.)

I *would* go if I were you.
(Again, the primary function of the auxiliary is to establish mood rather than tense.)

May and *might* are also used often to signify mood, as are *can* and *could*.

He *may* study tonight.

He *might* study tonight.
(In these sentences both forms refer to the same time. The second form, *might,* rather than indicating a different tense, signifies a lesser degree of probability than the first form, *may*.)

He *can* be an outstanding student.

He *could* be an outstanding student.
(Again, the auxiliaries refer not so much to time as to the degree of probability, *could* indicating a lesser degree.)

Despite the increasing use of these auxiliaries to replace the old subjunctive forms, however, they also continue to perform their other function of inflecting to indicate time relationships among verbs.

We *believe* that we *can* win.
may
will

We *believed* that we *could* win.
might
would

(In these examples the verbs *can, may,* and *will* change form to be in accord with the tense of the verb in the main clause. In this regard, they may be said to inflect to show tense. At the same time they also indicate, in both forms, that the verb in the dependent clause is in the subjunctive mood.)

Do clearly inflects to show tense, although it can signify only the present and past tenses.

He *does* need a haircut.
(Does indicates the present tense.)

He *did* need a haircut.
(*Did* indicates the past tense.)

In addition to the uses above, auxiliary verbs can be used to ask questions.

Can you swim?

Do you know the answer?

Has he been invited?

May I leave?

Shall I drive?

Will you go?

Tense Combinations

When there are two or more clauses in a sentence, the tenses that are used should indicate the correct time relationship among the verbs. There are usually several variations possible, and you should choose the combination that best indicates the time relationship that you intend. In the following sentence, for instance, several variations are possible:

He *says* that he *is* sick.
was sick.
has been sick.

No one of these is any better than the others. The choice depends upon what you want to say.

Notice also that when there are two or more clauses in a sentence, the tense used in the dependent clauses is governed to some extent by the tense used in the main clause. For instance, if the verb in the main clause is in the present tense, some tenses are possible in the dependent clause (or clauses), but others are not.

He *says* that the course *is* easy.
was easy.
will be easy.
has been easy.
but not *had been* easy.

On the other hand, if the verb in the main clause is in the past tense, the possible combinations will be different:

He *said* that the course *was* easy.
had been easy.
but probably not *is* easy
or *will be* easy.
(It is possible, however, to write "He said that the course *is* easy" if the statement is intended not as a comment on a

particular class but as a general truth about a standard course that is given regularly.)

Generally, more choices of tense are possible in a dependent clause if the main verb is in the present tense or future tense, and fewer choices are possible if the main verb is in the past tense or in one of the perfect tenses.

Since the tense of verbs is not the only way of indicating time in an English sentence, it is difficult to make rules for tense relationships that will apply in all circumstances. There are too many variables.

Time relationships may also be indicated to some extent by subordinate conjunctions *(after, before, since, until, when),* by adverbs *(then, recently, yesterday, tomorrow),* or by nouns naming time periods used with adjectives such as *next* or *last* (*next Tuesday, last summer,* etc.)

Notice, for instance, that the tense of the verbs is exactly the same in the two following sentences, yet because of a change in the subordinate conjunction the time relationship is different.

I went home before John arrived.

I went home when John arrived.

Notice also that the normal time reference of a particular tense form may actually be changed by the context in which it appears.

He will leave before the rush hour traffic *has begun.*
(Although *has begun* has the form of the present perfect tense, it actually refers to a future time here.)

Foyt will be exhausted when the race *ends.*
(In this case, the present tense form, *ends,* refers to a future time.)

Tense is so deeply embedded in our ways of thinking that tense combinations will usually evolve naturally from what you intend to say. But you should be aware that often there are several possible variations which may provide subtle differences of meaning.

Common Problems

1. Incorrect form of the past participle and the past tense. One simple error that occurs frequently is the omission of necessary endings for past participles, particularly the omission of the final *-ed*. Sometimes this is simply caused by haste. If so, it can be caught by careful proofreading and corrected before the paper is submitted. But with some verbs the problem is caused by uncertainty about the correct form of the past participle.

The following participles, in particular, are troublesome: *supposed, used, passed.*

We were *supposed to* (not *suppose to*) leave at eight o'clock.

We *used to* (not *use to*) study together every night.

I *passed* (not *past*) Frank on the street without recognizing him.

Some irregular verbs are especially troublesome in the selection of the proper form of the past participle and the past tense.

I *have seen* (not *have saw*) several good programs on PBS recently.

She *has begun* (not *has began*) a new career.

I *have swum* (not *have swam*) in the lake several times this summer.

He *has drunk* (not *has drank*) all the scotch.

Here is a list of the principal parts of other irregular verbs that are likely to cause problems in the selection of the correct form for the past tense or the past participle.

Present	*Past*	*Past Participle*
bear	bore	borne
blow	blew	blown
choose	chose	chosen
draw	drew	drawn
drive	drove	driven
eat	ate	eaten
fling	flung	flung
go	went	gone
grow	grew	grown
hear	heard	heard
know	knew	known
lead	led	led
lay	laid	laid
lie	lay	lain
pay	paid	paid
ride	rode	ridden
ring	rang	rung
rise	rose	risen
run	ran	run
shake	shook	shaken
show	showed	shown
shrink	shrank	shrunk
sing	sang	sung
sling	slung	slung
steal	stole	stolen
take	took	taken
tear	tore	torn
throw	threw	thrown
wring	wrung	wrung
write	wrote	written

2. Unnecessary shifts in tense. Once you have begun using one tense in a short paper or paragraph, you should continue to use that tense throughout, although you may of course shift temporarily to another tense if you have a good reason for doing so. The principle to follow is this: Do not shift tense needlessly. If you do shift tenses within a paragraph or between paragraphs, you should make sure that the reader will not be confused by the changed time reference. The transition from one time to another should be smooth and easy to follow.

UNNECESSARY SHIFT

Cruising along the coast of Africa, Marlowe has an impression of the enigmatic vastness of the continent and of the puny efforts of Europeans to subdue it. He sees settlements "no bigger than pinheads" in the vast expanse of jungle. He *saw* a ship firing futilely at the continent.

(The shift to the past tense, *saw,* in the last sentence is unnecessary. The writer could have written in the past tense from the beginning, but once he decided to begin with the present tense *(has, sees),* he should have continued to use it throughout the passage until he had a good reason for doing otherwise.)

3. Verb combinations with the auxiliary *would.* Many writers overuse *would.* As a general rule, when *would* is used in combination with *have* in the main clause, it is not used again in a dependent clause in the same sentence.

The ball would have cleared the fence if the wind *had been blowing* (not *would have been blowing*) in another direction.

If he *had been* (not *would have been*) more alert, the accident would not have occurred.

If it *had rained* (not *would have rained*) the game would have been cancelled.

Some writers also have a tendency to use *would have* unnecessarily in dependent clauses when *could have* is used in the main clause.

CORRECT

We could have won, if we *had followed* (not *would have followed*) our game plan.

4. The tense of infinitives. Infinitives have only two tenses: the present and the perfect. These tenses may be in the active or the passive voice.

	Active	*Passive*
Present	to see	to be seen
Perfect	to have seen	to have been seen

Use the perfect tense of the infinitive only if you want to indicate a time prior to the time of the main verb; otherwise use the present tense.

I am pleased *to meet you.*
(You might say this as you are introduced to someone.)

I am pleased *to have met you.*
(You might say this as you are leaving a party after having been introduced to someone earlier.)

Many writers are uncertain about what tense of the infinitive to use when the infinitive follows a verb that contains an auxiliary verb such as *would.* You should simply follow the rule given above. Use the present infinitive unless you want to indicate a time prior to that of the main verb.

He would like *to see* (not *to have seen*) you.

He would have liked *to see* (not *to have seen*) you.

5. The tense of participles. Like infinitives, participles have only two tenses: the present and the perfect. Normally only participles based on verbs that can be used transitively have a passive voice.

	Active	*Passive*
Present	seeing	being seen
Perfect	having seen	having been seen
Present	sleeping	(Since sleep cannot be used transitively,
Perfect	having slept	it has no passive participle.)

Generally, the rule for the tense of infinitives also applies to participles: Use the perfect participle only if you want to indicate a time prior to the time of the main verb; otherwise use the present participle. The present participle is used, however, if the times expressed by the participle and by the main verb are almost simultaneous even though the time of the participle logically precedes the time of the main verb.

> *Having experienced* the horrors of war, he *became* an avid pacifist.
> (His experience of war preceded his becoming a pacifist.)
>
> *Having realized* that he was late, he *began* to drive faster.
>
> *Realizing* that he was late, he *began* to drive faster.
> (Although the first version of this sentence follows the general rule, the second version is also acceptable and would probably be preferable. The choice would depend on whether you wanted to indicate a slight delay between the act of realizing and the act of speeding or whether you wanted to indicate that they occurred almost simultaneously.)

Looking across the desert, he *sees* a distant trail of dust.

Looking across the desert, he *saw* a distant trail of dust.
(The present participle may be used in either version because the actions of looking and seeing are almost simultaneous, regardless of the tense of the main verb.)

Remember that the present participle is used much more frequently than the perfect participle. Also remember that a choice between the present and perfect participle depends not on the tense of the main verb but on the time relationship between the participle and the main verb.

G 8 VOICE

Verbs may be inflected to show active or passive voice.

If the subject does the action described by the verb or if the subject is simply joined to a complement by a linking verb, the verb is in the **active** voice. If the subject is the receiver of the action described by the verb, the verb is in the **passive** voice. Only transitive verbs may be used in the passive voice.

ACTIVE VOICE (TRANSITIVE VERB)

We *ate* the cake.
(The subject, *we,* does the action described by the verb. The direct object, *cake,* receives the action.)

ACTIVE VOICE (LINKING VERB)

The cake *was* good.
(The subject, *cake,* is linked to a predicate adjective, *good,* by the verb. The passive voice cannot be used with a linking verb.)

ACTIVE VOICE (INTRANSITIVE VERB)

The cake *fell.*
(The subject, *cake,* does the action described by the verb.

There is no complement. The passive voice cannot be used with an intransitive verb.)

PASSIVE VOICE (TRANSITIVE VERB)

The cake *was eaten.*
(In this sentence the subject, *cake,* receives the action described by the verb. There is no complement.)

The verbs in the examples above are all in the past tense, but there is a different form for the active and passive voices in each of the six tenses. For a comparison of the forms for the active and passive voices in each of the tenses, see the conjugation of the verb *see* on pages 19–21.

Although the passive voice is sometimes preferable to the active voice, especially when the actor is less important than the receiver of the action or when the actor is unknown (e.g., Lincoln was inaugurated on March 4, 1861), the active voice produces greater stylistic force and is generally preferable to the passive.

WEAK PASSIVE VOICE

A better day for the game *could not have been asked for.*

ACTIVE VOICE

We could not have asked for a better day for the game.

or

The day broke cold and clear, with no wind to interfere with passes or high punts.

WEAK PASSIVE

The flashing light *was not heeded* by Sue.

ACTIVE VOICE

Sue *ignored* the flashing light.

WEAK PASSIVE

A thorough investigation of every accident *is conducted* by the highway patrol.

ACTIVE VOICE

The highway patrol *conducts* a thorough investigation of every accident.

Sentence Structure

You have been *speaking* sentences for many years without being especially conscious of what you were doing. And many of those sentences have been very effective. But spoken sentences are not quite the same as written ones. For one thing, they do not have to be as exact. They can be broken off or changed in mid-course without a loss of communication. They can be supplemented by shrugs, smiles, a raised or lowered voice, or an emphatic intonation, and if the listener doesn't seem to understand, they can be quickly changed and explained further. In written sentences, however, the quick give and take of ordinary conversation is lost, and you have to take care to express your meaning more exactly. In other words, you have to respond to a reader's difficulties *before* he has them by making your meaning unmistakable—or as nearly so as you can. This is not always easy, but the first step is to realize that frequently there is a discrepancy between your thoughts and what you actually write down. What is written is usually a *reduction* of the many thoughts and attitudes that are running through your mind. The reader, however, is aware only of the actual words on the page and the meaning they convey. You cannot assume that the words have all the associations for him that they have for you, because he comes to them in a different way, without the chain of associations, random thoughts, and emotions that preceded your writing them. Therefore, once you have written them, or even while writing them if you can, you need to undertake the difficult task of thinking as a writer and as a reader at the same time, changing any sentences or parts of sentences that you can make better from either perspective.

Good sentences sometimes just happen, without anyone—including the writer—being quite sure why or how. The mind works in mysterious ways, and we are thankful when it provides a sentence that we would not want to change. But more often than not, good sentences take form gradually and with concentrated effort. They are not only a focusing of thought; they are verbal artifacts, things made. And it helps a great deal if you have some knowledge of *how* they are made. The pages that follow can help make you a more conscious reader and writer of sentences and can assist you (in the numbered entries at the end of the section) with particular problems that commonly cause difficulties.

Building Sentences

THE SENTENCE LINE: SUBJECTS, VERBS, AND COMPLEMENTS

A written sentence in English is clearly linear, moving in time and space from the first word to the last, from left to right in lines, across the page. The primary ordering principle of the sentence is that the *subject, verb* and *complement* usually appear in a certain predictable order. The subject, as a general rule, comes first, followed by the verb, and then by the complement, if there is one. The order in which these basic elements occur indicates their relationship. For instance, although the same words are used in the two following sentences, the change in the order in which they occur changes their relationship to each other and therefore changes their meaning.

John hit the ball.

The ball hit John.
(In the first sentence *John* is the subject and *ball* is the complement, in this case a direct object. In the second sentence *ball* is the subject and John is the direct object. The verb is, of course, the same in both sentences.)

Notice, however, that not all changes would be meaningful. The following sentences, for example, have no clear meaning:

John the hit ball.

Ball John the hit.

The use of word order to indicate the relationship of the parts of the sentence is so basic that most writers use it automatically, but the subject-verb-complement base is capable of many complex variations, some of which can cause problems, even for experienced writers.

Rather than analyzing sentences, let's try our hand at *building* sentences.

Perhaps the first step in perceiving how sentences fit together is to understand the importance of verbs.

There are three kinds of verbs: **transitive, linking,** and **intransitive**. (If necessary, consult the List of Terms, p. 200 ff.)

Transitive Verbs

Transitive verbs may be used in either the active or the passive voice.

In the active voice, a transitive verb requires a complement* called a direct object to complete the statement begun by the subject and the verb. Let's take a sentence using a transitive verb in the active voice and watch it in slow motion as it takes form.

SUBJECT

The wind . . .

SUBJECT + TRANSITIVE VERB

The wind scattered . . .

SUBJECT + TRANSITIVE VERB + DIRECT OBJECT

The wind scattered the leaves.

You might have stopped with the verb if you were using an intransitive verb, as in the following sentences:

The wind died.

The wind rose.

But a sentence with a transitive verb in the active voice obviously

*The most common complements are direct objects, indirect objects, predicate adjectives, and predicate nouns.

needs something following the verb to complete the meaning. You would not, for instance, say "The wind scattered . . ." or "The wind scattered the . . ." However, once a direct object is supplied, in this case *leaves,* there is a sense of completion. The statement might be elaborated by the addition of modifiers, but the basic structure of the sentence is completed with the addition of the direct object.

All three parts (subject, transitive verb, direct object) are essential, but notice that the verb relates in both directions (to the subject, which precedes it, and to the direct object, which follows it) whereas the other two parts relate to each other only through the verb. If the verb were omitted ("The wind . . . the leaves"), the relationship of the other two parts would not be clear.

Some constructions using transitive active verbs require an indirect object as well as a direct object. Again, let's look at an example in slow motion:

SUBJECT

Fred . . .

SUBJECT + TRANSITIVE VERB

Fred handed . . .

SUBJECT + TRANSITIVE VERB + DIRECT OBJECT

Fred handed the book . . .

In this case, although you have a subject, a transitive verb, and a direct object, the statement still seems incomplete. Something else is needed.

There are two ways to handle this problem:

1. You may add a prepositional phrase *after* the direct object:

Fred handed the book *to me*.

or

2. You may add an indirect object *between* the verb and the direct object:

Fred handed *me* the book.
(*Me* is the indirect object.)

In the passive voice, a transitive verb has no need of a direct (or indirect) object to receive the action. Instead, the subject receives the action.

The leaves were scattered by the wind.
(*Leaves,* which is now the subject, receives the action expressed by the verb. *Wind,* which was the subject in the version of this sentence given earlier, has been made the object of the preposition *by*.)

Only transitive verbs may be used in the passive voice. Linking verbs and intransitive verbs are used in the active voice only.

Linking Verbs

A linking verb serves primarily as a structural link between a subject and a complement such as a predicate adjective or a predicate noun, or, in some instances, between a subject and a prepositional phrase.

Let's watch a sentence with a linking verb as it takes form:

SUBJECT

Frank . . .

SUBJECT + LINKING VERB

Frank is . . .

Again, a complement is needed to complete the statement, but this time several kinds of complements are possible:

Frank is *nervous*.
(A predicate adjective, *nervous,* follows the linking verb.)

Frank is an avid *reader.*
(A predicate noun, *reader,* follows the linking verb.)

Frank is *in the house.*
(A prepositional phrase, *in the house,* follows the linking verb.)

Note: In addition to various inflections of the verb *be* (*is, are, am, was, have been,* etc.), a number of other verbs may be used as linking verbs. Some examples are *seem, appear, feel, become.*

Linking verbs are also used with delayed subjects, when an expletive precedes the verb and the subject follows the verb:

EXPLETIVE

There . . .

EXPLETIVE + LINKING VERB

There is . . .

EXPLETIVE + LINKING VERB + DELAYED SUBJECT

There is a *storm* near the coast.
(In this construction the subject, *storm,* comes after the verb instead of preceding it.)

In constructions with delayed subjects, a modifying phrase or clause is usually needed to complete the full meaning, as in these sentences:

There is a reason *for his anger.*
(The phrase *for his anger* is needed to complete the meaning.)

There are places *where the sun never shines.*
(In this sentence a clause, *where the sun never shines,* completes the meaning.)

Intransitive Verbs

An intransitive verb does not require a complement. The statement which the sentence makes is essentially completed by the subject and the verb, although modifiers may, of course, be used to elaborate or refine the statement.

Susan smiled.

John snored.

The kite fell.
(Nothing is needed after the verb, although modifiers could be added either before or after the verb.)

Notice that some verbs may be either transitive or intransitive, depending on how they are used in particular sentences. The way that they are used is more important than the fact that they are spelled alike.

The play *began*.
(*Began* does not need a complement here. It is intransitive.)

The starter's gun *began* the race.
(*Began* is followed by a direct object, *race*. The verb is transitive.)

VARYING AND EXPANDING THE SENTENCE LINE

Most of the examples so far have been short and simple in order to emphasize the importance of subjects, verbs, and complements. Now let us consider how the subject-verb-complement base may be expanded and varied.

Using Modifiers

Modifiers may be added to subjects, verbs, or complements.

These modifiers may be words, phrases, or dependent clauses.* Modifiers—regardless of whether they are words, phrases, or clauses—are used as either adjectives or adverbs.

SINGLE WORDS

The *lone* horseman rode *westward.*
(*Lone* is an adjective modifying the subject *horseman. Westward* is an adverb modifying the verb *rode.*)

PHRASES

The snow *on the mountains* will provide water *in the spring.*
(The prepositional phrase *on the mountains* is used as an adjective modifying the subject *snow.* The prepositional phrase *in the spring* is used as an adverb modifying the verb *will provide.*)

Slipping on the ice, he struggled *to keep his balance.*
(The participial phrase *slipping on the ice* is used as an adjective modifying the subject *he*. The infinitive phrase *to keep his balance* is used as an adverb modifying the verb *struggled.* Notice that without the modifiers the sentence would read simply *He struggled.* The modifiers provide an important part of the meaning of the sentence.)

DEPENDENT CLAUSES

The steel beams, *which are so prominent now,* will not be seen *when the building is completed.*
(The *which* clause is used as an adjective modifying the subject *beams.* The *when* clause is used as an adverb modifying the verb *will be seen.*)

Stabler threw a long pass, *which Biletnikoff caught in the end zone.*
(The *which* clause modifies the direct object, *pass.*)

---

*Consult the List of Terms, p. 200, if necessary.

The placement of modifiers is important in establishing their relationship to the words they modify. The general principle is that adjectives should be placed as near as possible to the words they modify, with adverbs sometimes, but not always, having more latitude in their placement along the sentence line.

Notice, for instance, the distortion of meaning which may occur if an adjective phrase is placed too far from the word it is intended to modify, as in the following sentence:

The bus pulled into the station *from Chicago*.
(The phrase *from Chicago* seems to modify the noun *station* although it is intended to modify *bus*.)

If the phrase is placed near the word it is intended to modify, however, the difficulty disappears.

The bus *from Chicago* pulled into the station.

There are usually a greater number of options in the placement of adverbs along the sentence line, but even with adverbs there are a limited number of possibilities. For instance, let's take four short sentences and observe at what points adverbs may be embedded within them.

In how many places in the following sentence can you place the adverb *slowly* without causing awkwardness?

He squeezed the trigger.

There are three placements which would cause no difficulty:

Slowly he squeezed the trigger.

He *slowly* squeezed the trigger.

He squeezed the trigger *slowly*.

You could not, however, place the adverb between the verb, *squeezed*, and the direct object, *trigger*, without causing awkwardness.

In how many places in the following sentence could you place the adverb *slowly?*

The image on the screen came into focus.

There are four possibilities:

Slowly the image on the screen came into focus.

The image on the screen *slowly* came into focus.

The image on the screen came *slowly* into focus.

The image on the screen came into focus *slowly*.

At what places in the following sentence could you place the adverbial phrase *on Thursday?*

Ms. Mengel asked us to visit the museum.

There are three possibilities:

On Thursday Ms. Mengel asked us to visit the museum.

Ms. Mengel asked us *on Thursday* to visit the museum.

Ms. Mengel asked us to visit the museum *on Thursday*.

Notice, however, that the meaning would not be the same in each of these three sentences. In the first two versions the phrase *on Thursday* would be assumed to modify the verb *asked,* but in the third version it would be assumed to modify the infinitive *to visit*.

In how many places could the dependent clause *when I fell* be embedded in the following sentence?

I lost my keys in the snow.

There are three possibilities:

When I fell, I lost my keys in the snow.

I lost my keys *when I fell* in the snow.

I lost my keys in the snow *when I fell*.

All of these sentences would be grammatically correct, but the meaning, or at least the emphasis, would be different in each sentence.

Using Phrases As Subjects, Complements, or Objects of Prepositions

In addition to being used as modifiers, phrases may be used as subjects, complements, or objects of prepositions.

A GERUND PHRASE USED AS A SUBJECT

Walking up stairs is a convenient form of exercise.

AN INFINITIVE PHRASE USED AS A SUBJECT

To err is human.

A GERUND PHRASE USED AS A PREDICATE NOUN

His favorite pastime is *watching television.*

A GERUND PHRASE USED AS A DIRECT OBJECT

Whitman heard *America Singing.*

AN INFINITIVE PHRASE USED AS A DIRECT OBJECT

Tom likes *to watch television.*

A GERUND PHRASE USED AS THE OBJECT OF A PREPOSITION

He is addicted to *watching television.*

Using Clauses As Subjects, Complements, or Objects of Prepositions

Dependent clauses may also be used as subjects, complements, or objects of prepositions. Such clauses usually begin with one of the following words: *who, what, that, whoever, whatever.*

A CLAUSE USED AS A SUBJECT

What happened next was a complete surprise.

That the weather forecast had been wrong was obvious.

Whoever wins will be champion.

A CLAUSE USED AS A PREDICATE NOUN

His price is *whatever the market will bear.*

A CLAUSE USED AS A DIRECT OBJECT

We knew *that the exam would be difficult.*

A CLAUSE USED AS THE OBJECT OF A PREPOSITION

He gave money to *whoever needed it.*

Doubling Parts of a Sentence

With very few exceptions, parts of a sentence may be doubled or even tripled by adding other parts of that same type. For example, there may be more than one subject, more than one verb, more than one direct object, or more than one adjective modifying the same word. These similar parts are said to be **coordinate**.

COORDINATE SUBJECTS

Rosencrantz and *Guildenstern* are dead.

COORDINATE VERBS

The radiator *hissed* menacingly, then *growled,* and finally *erupted.*

COORDINATE PREDICATE ADJECTIVES

His approach was *slow* and *easy.*

COORDINATE PREDICATE NOUNS

The only four states whose boundaries intersect at a common point are *Arizona, Utah, Colorado,* and *New Mexico.*

COORDINATE DIRECT OBJECTS

Statistics indifferently offer cunning *lies* or brutal *truths*.

He knew *what she liked, what she merely tolerated,* and *what she abhorred*.

COORDINATE ADJECTIVES

The *cool, translucent* water soon filled the glass.

COORDINATE PREPOSITIONAL PHRASES

The dust seeped *under the window sill, across the room,* and *into the food*.

She looked not quite *at* him, but *over, through,* and *around* him.
(This is an extreme example, but it does make the point that even short function words like prepositions can be coordinate, in this case quadrupally so.)

In addition to coordination within clauses, as in the examples above, clauses may be coordinate to each other. Any independent clause* is considered to be structurally coordinate or equal to any other independent clause, regardless of differences in length. Thus, when two or more independent clauses appear in the same sentence, they are said to be coordinate.

COORDINATE CLAUSES

Ice was forming in the puddles, but *the sun was shining*.
(Two independent clauses are linked by the coordinate conjunction *but*.)

Of course, independent clauses can also be combined with dependent clauses. When such a combination is used, the dependent clauses are said to be *subordinate* to the independent clauses. Frequently you will have the choice of making a clause either

*Consult the List of Terms, p. 203, if necessary.

subordinate or coordinate to another clause. For instance, one of the independent clauses in the example above could be subordinated to the other, as in this version:

> Although ice was forming in the puddles, the sun was shining.
> (The use of the subordinate conjunction *although* indicates that the first clause is subordinate to the second one. For further examples of coordinate and subordinate conjunctions, see *Conjunction* in the List of Terms, p. 205).

See S 5 and S 6, pp. 64–68.

Using Appositives

Subjects, direct objects, and predicate nouns (as well as substantives* in modifying clauses and phrases) may have appositives* which are coordinate to them.

> Mount Everest, *the world's highest elevation,* is 29,028 feet above sea level.
> (*The world's highest elevation* is in apposition with the subject, *Mount Everest.*)

> He has read only one book, the *Sears Roebuck Catalogue.*
> (The *Sears Roebuck Catalogue* is in apposition with the direct object, *book.*)

> His favorite drink is a boilermaker, *a potent mixture of beer and whiskey.*
> (*Mixture,* with its modifiers, is in apposition with the predicate noun, *boilermaker.*)

For further examples of appositives, see p. 52.

---

*See the List of Terms, pp. 202, 221, if necessary.

BEGINNINGS, MIDDLES, AND ENDINGS

Beginnings

You will have noticed from some of the examples above that a sentence does not have to begin invariably with the subject. Let's experiment with some possible ways of beginning a sentence.

Using one of the topics on pp. 225–232, write a series of sentences that begin with the following constructions:

1. A prepositional phrase (for instance, *In* . . .)
2. A participial phrase (*Standing* . . .)
3. A dependent clause (*Although* . . .)
4. An adverb (*Suddenly* . . .)
5. Anything else (except the subject) that comes to mind

There are other ways of beginning sentences, as a close examination of a number of specimen sentences will reveal, but the first four patterns above offer serviceable alternatives to beginning with the subject. You will no doubt discover others in response to number 5.

Middles

Occasionally, effects of special emphasis can be achieved in the Subject-Verb-Complement pattern by delaying or suspending the completion of the pattern.

s *v* *c*
Lawyers, I suppose, were children once. Charles Lamb

s *v* *c*
Weather, of course, is an obsession with the television people. E. B. White

s *v* *c*
John, who had always wanted a Mercedes, bought a Honda.

(In all three sentences, intervening phrases or clauses are placed between the subject and the verb, momentarily suspending the completion of the s-v-c pattern.)

s *v*
John wrote, to his instructor's surprise, a brilliant final
c
examination.
(In this case the suspension is between the verb and the complement.)

Appositives, as well as qualifying phrases and clauses, can be used to create suspension—especially when they are placed in the middle of a statement.

Shakespeare, the greatest writer in our language, has the largest vocabulary of any English author.

Of course, appositives can also be placed at the end of sentences, where the emphasis is somewhat different.

The pitcher, immobile on the mound, holds the inert white ball, his little lump of physics. Roger Angell

Endings

Because of the terminal pause and the sense of completion, words at the end of a sentence tend to receive emphasis. This will not happen automatically, however. Some sentences merely dribble to weak and inconsequential endings, and others may be deliberately subordinated to a prior emphasis in the sentence. Occasionally, however, you may want to exploit the possibilities of the final position by building toward an emphatic conclusion.

There is only one person whom he admires without reservation: himself.

(In this sentence the terminal pause is further intensified by the pause after the colon, throwing a strong final emphasis upon the word *himself.*)

A discouraging number of reputable poets are sane beyond recall. E. B. White

(The completion of the basic thought of this short sentence is delayed until the word *sane,* but it is not quite completed there. The concluding phrase adds a final emphasis.)

The emphasis need not always be upon a major structural element, such as a complement or a verb, nor does it have to be as strong as in the first example given. The following sentence, for instance, ends with a moderate stress upon a word in a modifying phrase.

At noon we sat outside, basking in the luxury of the warm sun.

The emphasis upon a particular word or phrase is seldom a matter of position or structure alone. The contextual relationship with other words in the sentence may be just as important. One reason, for instance, that the phrase *the warm sun* stands out in the sentence above is the relationship between it and the other words in the sentence. The words in the main clause are short, simple words with very little connotative charge, and their relative neutrality serves as a foil for the stronger connotations of words like *basking, luxury,* and *the warm sun*. Also, the final emphasis upon *the warm sun* is strengthened by the favorable connotations of *basking* and *luxury,* which lead up to it.

IMPROVING YOUR SKILLS

Here are some exercises to familiarize you, through practice, with some of the basic patterns used in forming sentences.

Combining Sentences

In each set of sentences below, combine the individual sentences to form one good sentence. In most of the sets you are given a hint to get you started. When no instructions are given, use your own judgment. Your sentences should be compared with those of your classmates if possible.

Exercise 1

Combine the sentences in the following sets by changing one of the sentences to a participial phrase or to a dependent clause, as instructed. For example, you might combine these two sentences

The hawk flew high above the canyon.

He seemed small.

into this sentence

Flying high above the canyon, the hawk seemed small.

or into this sentence

As he flew high above the canyon, the hawk seemed small.

1. Smith sprinted around the final turn.
   He gradually increased his lead.
   (Use a participial phrase.)
2. A commercial appears on his television set.
   He quickly changes channels.
   (Use a dependent clause.)
3. He gave a name.
   The name was not his own.
   (Use a dependent clause.)
4. Namath looked at his knee.
   He knew that this would be his last game.
   (Use a participial phrase.)

5. Snow fell all night.
   It covered the city's hard geometry.
   (Use a participial phrase.)

Exercise 2

Combine the sentences in the following sets, using the pattern suggested for each set.

1. It is obvious.
   Everyone is concerned about inflation.
   (Use a *that* clause.)
2. Frank realized it.
   The exam would be difficult.
   (Use a *that* clause.)
3. I predict something.
   Our team will win.
   (Use a *that* clause.)
4. I expect something.
   Our team will win.
   (Use an infinitive phrase.)
5. He said something.
   I was surprised by it.
   (Use any pattern that seems appropriate.)

Exercise 3

Combine the sentences in the sets below, following the suggestions given. When no suggestions are provided, use any pattern that seems appropriate.

1. Simpson broke through the middle.
   He veered to the right.
   He raced down the sidelines.
   (Use a series of verbs and prepositional phrases.)

2. He knew the price of everything.
   He knew the value of nothing.
   (Use *but*.)
3. Oswald was being escorted through the crowd.
   A shot rang out.
4. Bain watched the receding back of the jailor.
   He took a cold steel bar in each hand.
   He waited.
   (Begin with a participle, *watching*.)
5. Only thirty-seven seconds of the first round had elapsed.
   Louis landed an uppercut to Schmelling's jaw.
   The fight was over.
   (Begin with *After*.)
6. A man is imprisoned.
   He may learn to understand freedom.
   A man is free.
   He cannot see his shackles.
   (Use *who* or *if* clauses, joined by *but*.)
7. Yarborough was running in second place.
   There were four laps to go.
   He decided not to make a pit stop.
   His fuel gauge registered empty.
   (Begin with a participle, *running*, and end with an *although* clause.)
8. It was thirteen degrees below zero in Green Bay.
   The game with Dallas was played as scheduled.
9. The faces in the photograph are young.
   They never change.
   They are frozen in time.
10. Helicopters do not have the range or the seating capacity of jets.

> Helicopters are more expensive to operate than automobiles.
> Helicopters are the most efficient means of transportation in some situations.
> They are especially useful in areas where there is heavy traffic congestion.
> They are also useful in areas where there are no landing facilities for larger aircraft.
> (Don't let the length or the number of these sentences overwhelm you. They can be combined to form one good sentence.)

As you know by now, there is more than one way to express the thought of a sentence. Look back at the sentences in which you were asked to use specified patterns and try to find other ways of combining them.

Copying Sentences

One of the best ways of learning what constitutes good sentences is also one of the simplest: copying. One problem in this regard is finding good sentences, or knowing when you have found one. Don't worry about it too much. Just start looking, and when you find a sentence that you like, copy it. The main thing is to sensitize yourself to sentences by looking at them closely. Just the act of searching for good sentences will cause you to examine them more closely than you have in the past. If you need help in getting started, your instructor will probably be glad to recommend particular authors or publications which are likely to provide good specimens, but you will find them all around you—sometimes in places which you might not have considered likely sources. *Organic Gardening,* for instance, usually contains many good sentences. So does *Rolling Stone.* And, if you look carefully, so do newspapers and weekly magazines.

Keep a place in one of your notebooks where you can collect

specimen sentences. When you find one that you especially like, copy it in longhand several times, but not too many times. When the process becomes boring and your mind begins to wander, it's time to stop. There is no value in the act of copying itself. The main value lies in your becoming aware of the rhythms and patterns of the sentences by repeating them in your own mind and handwriting until you get a sense of the way they flow together, of their wholeness. You might even try memorizing a sentence and repeating it to yourself from time to time during the day.

Once you have accumulated a number of individual sentences in your notebook, you can start looking for groups of sentences or paragraphs. Copy them in your notebook too, noticing how the sentences work together.

Common Problems in Sentences

The following pages discuss some of the problems most frequently encountered in writing sentences and suggest ways of dealing with them.

S 1 FRAGMENT

A fragment is an incomplete sentence punctuated as though it were a complete sentence.

A skilled writer sometimes may use fragments deliberately, for emphasis or contrast. The student, however, should use them only when he can justify their use. There is rarely any justification for punctuating a single thought as though it were two sentences, as in this example:

FRAGMENT

He settled comfortably on the grass. Listening to the music. (The second "sentence" is incomplete by itself.)

REVISED

He settled comfortably on the grass, listening to the music.

Settling comfortably on the grass, he listened to the music.

He settled comfortably on the grass and listened to the music.

Notice, however, that the four words "listening to the music" receive much more emphasis in the fragment than they do when incorporated into a sentence. There is some justification for a fragment if you have deliberately chosen to emphasize the words in the fragment. If you decide to use a fragment in a theme, be prepared to justify your choice. Remember also that such constructions lose their effectiveness if they are used too often.

S 2 DANGLING MODIFIER

1. Dangling participle. A participial phrase which cannot logically modify any word in a sentence, or which seems to modify a word it obviously is not intended to modify, is said to dangle. Participles at the beginning of a sentence seem to cause the most trouble, but dangling participles may cause confusion in the middle or at the end of the sentence as well.

One can correct a dangling participial phrase in two ways: (1) by supplying a noun or pronoun which the phrase can logically modify; (2) by changing the participial phrase to a dependent clause.

DANGLING

Kissing her passionately, the car ran off the road.
(Is the car doing the kissing?)

REVISED

Kissing her passionately, he lost control of the car.
(The participial phrase clearly modifies the pronoun *he*.)

As he kissed her passionately, the car ran off the road.
(The participial phrase is changed to a dependent clause.)

DANGLING

We missed the train, *causing us to be late.*
(There is no word in the sentence that the phrase *causing us to be late* can logically modify.)

REVISED

We were late because we missed the train.

2. Dangling gerund. Since gerunds retain some of the characteristics of verbs, there must be some word in the sentence which is capable of performing the action described by the gerund. When there is no such word in the sentence, the gerund is said to dangle.

DANGLING

After reading for two hours, my book dropped to the floor. (The book seems to have done the reading.)

REVISED

After reading for two hours, I fell asleep.

After I had read for two hours, my book dropped to the floor.

S 3 MISPLACED MODIFIER

Modifiers should be placed near the words they are intended to modify. Otherwise they may seem to modify the wrong word.

MISPLACED MODIFIER

A car was parked in front of the house *with a dented fender.*

REVISED

A car *with a dented fender* was parked in front of the house.

MISPLACED MODIFIER

The comedian *nearly* entertained us for two hours.

REVISED

The comedian entertained us for *nearly* two hours.

S 4 PARALLELISM

Parallel constructions are parts of a sentence that are similar in form, as in the familiar phrase "a government *of the people, by the people, for the people,*" with its three parallel prepositional phrases. If coordinate parts of the sentence are made closely alike in form, their relationship will be more immediately obvious and the thought will flow more smoothly. Notice, for example, these two sentences:

NOT PARALLEL

Sleeping and *when he was awake,* he dreamed of her.
(The word *and* joins coordinate thoughts, but here they are not parallel in form.)

PARALLEL

Sleeping and *waking,* he dreamed of her.

The coordinate parts don't always have to be exactly alike, but they should be similar enough for their relationship to be easily understood.

NOT PARALLEL

He wanted to know *who wrote the book and its cost.*

NOT EXACTLY PARALLEL, BUT CLEAR

He wanted to know who wrote the book and how much it cost.

Repetition of Key Words

The effect of parallel constructions can often be heightened by the repetition of key words, as in the following sentence.

Watching the graceful young athletes, the old man remembered *other* afternoons and *other* players.
(Notice the difference in effect if the sentence is read without the repetition of *other.*)

Sometimes repetition of key structural words is necessary to avoid confusion or awkwardness.

AWKWARD

John went to the library and the bookstore, but not class.

REVISED

John went *to* the library and *to* the bookstore, but not *to* class.
(The second *to* is optional in this case.)

For further examples of necessary repetition, see S 12.

Parallelism with Correlative Conjunctions

Place correlative conjunctions (*not only . . . but also, both . . . and, either . . . or, neither . . . nor*) so that the part of the sentence coming after the first conjunction is similar (i.e., parallel) to the part coming after the second conjunction.

NOT PARALLEL

Either he was a liar *or* an imbecile.
(The first correlative is followed by a clause, the second by a noun.)

PARALLEL

He was *either* a liar *or* an imbecile.
(Each correlative is followed by a noun.)

NOT PARALLEL

Coach Smith hopes *both* to have a good season *and* expects to.

PARALLEL

Coach Smith *both* hopes *and* expects to have a good season.

NOT PARALLEL

Rueschel pitched *not only* a perfect game *but also* hit a home run.

PARALLEL

Rueschel *not only* pitched a perfect game *but also* hit a home run.

The following paragraph by John F. Kennedy is a good example of the use of parallelism. Study it closely, identifying as many parallel constructions as you can.

> Those who came before us made certain that this country rode the first waves of the industrial revolution, the first waves of modern invention and the first wave of nuclear power, and this generation does not intend to founder in the backwash of the coming age of space. We mean to be a part of it. We mean to lead it, for the eyes of the world now look into space, to the moon and to the planets beyond; and we have vowed that we shall not see it governed by a hostile flag of conquest, but by a banner of freedom and peace. We have vowed that we shall not see space filled with weapons of mass destruction, but with instruments of knowledge and understanding.

S 5 COORDINATION

If you tend to use coordinate clauses too frequently, you should consider the possibility of subordinating one or more of the clauses when you find yourself writing a series of coordinate clauses. In particular, be alert for the excessive use of constructions such as the following:

1. Indiscriminate coordination. Don't use coordination when the relationship between clauses can be shown more clearly by subordinating one of them.

COORDINATE CLAUSES

The rain began, and we were walking along the highway.

SUBORDINATED

When the rain began, we were walking along the highway.

COORDINATE CLAUSES

There was a long delay, and the passengers were angry.

SUBORDINATED

The passengers were angered by the long delay.

2. Primer sentences. The use of many short simple sentences in succession creates the impression that the thought of each sentence is of equal importance. The thought will flow more smoothly and the relationship between the sentences will be clearer if some of the sentences are subordinated.

PRIMER SENTENCES

The wind was blowing. It was cold. The fields were covered with snow. I left the house.

IMPROVED BY SUBORDINATION

A cold wind was blowing across the snow-covered fields as I left the house.

3. Excessive coordinate conjunctions. Excessive use of coordinate conjunctions such as *and, or,* or *but* creates the impression of a stringing together of phrases and clauses with no indication of their relative importance. The thought can usually be stated more clearly and more concisely through subordinating one or more of the coordinate elements.

EXCESSIVE COORDINATION

The car hit the wall *and* careened down the track *and* began to come apart *and* a wheel rolled slowly past it *and* various pieces of metal lay scattered in its wake, *and* then it rolled to a stop *and* began to burn.

IMPROVED BY SUBORDINATION

As the car hit the wall and careened down the track, it began to come apart. Various pieces of metal lay scattered in its wake, and a wheel slowly rolled past as it came to a stop and began to burn.

S 6 SUBORDINATION

Although subordination may help you to improve the subtlety and precision of your sentences, if it is used carelessly it may cause more problems than it solves. Beware of the following careless uses of subordination:

1. Misplaced subordination. Sometimes a thought may be placed in either an independent clause or a subordinate construction without a significant variation in its meaning.

> Fisher moved his queen decisively, checkmating his opponent.
>
> *or*
>
> Moving his queen decisively, Fisher checkmated his opponent.

There is a slight difference of emphasis in these two sentences, but the meaning is essentially the same in either version.

In many instances, however, the placement of an important idea or detail in a subordinate construction can distort your meaning or create an unintended emphasis. Be sure that the structure reinforces the meaning and emphasis that you want.

> MISPLACED SUBORDINATION
>
> When I lost my keys, I fell in the snow.
>
> REVISED
>
> I lost my keys when I fell in the snow.
>
> MISPLACED SUBORDINATION
>
> Simpson broke into the clear as he tripped and fell.
> (There is a distortion of sequence as well as of emphasis here. The culminating action in time and in importance should be the tripping and falling.)

REVISED

As he broke into the clear, Simpson tripped and fell.

or

Breaking into the clear, Simpson tripped and fell.

MISPLACED SUBORDINATION

When the hostage dashed to safety, the police distracted the hijacker.

REVISED

When the police distracted the hijacker, the hostage dashed to safety.

2. Excessive subordination. Like any good thing, subordination can be overused—usually when a sentence is overloaded with too many qualifications or too many inconsequential details. The main point of your sentence should be clear and easily followed. Anything that obscures the primary thought should be eliminated.

Although most of our cities are clogged by traffic because of our insistence on driving our own cars everywhere, despite the inefficiency of such transportation, there has been little effort to improve public transportation in this country, except in a few cities like San Francisco and Chicago, and more recently, Washington, D.C., where the new metro system is near completion, although it takes years to get a mass transportation system from the planning stages into actual operation, and we need relief from the congestion in our cities now.

(The central idea of this sentence is hidden beneath a mass of qualifications and unnecessary details. As a general rule, it is a good practice to use no more than one or two qualifying clauses in a sentence, or at least to use no more than the reader can absorb without strain. If many complex qualifications come to mind, develop some of them in additional sentences.)

REVISED

Although most of our cities need relief from traffic congestion, there has been no concerted effort to improve public transportation in this country.
(Some of the details and qualifications could be included in further sentences.)

S 7 AWKWARD CONSTRUCTION

Sometimes a sentence may be so awkwardly phrased or so confusing that it must be rewritten, even though it is grammatically correct. If ony a part of the sentence is awkward or slightly awkward in its phrasing, your instructor may have underlined the problem area, and sometimes you can concentrate on rephrasing only that part of the sentence. Frequently, however, patching up one part of a sentence throws something else out of kilter. The best procedure is usually to clarify in your own mind what you intended to say and then to rephrase the whole sentence as clearly and simply as possible.

Here are a few awkward sentences:

AWKWARD

When I first came to the university I didn't think I was going to like it as well as I thought I would.

REVISED

When I first came to the university I didn't like it as well as I had thought I would.

AWKWARD

People who smoke cigars consist almost entirely of businessmen.

REVISED

Most of the cigar smokers that I know are businessmen.

AWKWARD

Dogs have been in our family for years, starting with Grandmother.

REVISED

We have had dogs in our family since my grandmother bought a Pekinese in 1945.

There are varying degrees of awkwardness, of course, and there are extreme examples. The point is that the writers of these sentences saw nothing wrong with them at the moment of composition.

All of us have at times written awkward sentences without being aware that they were awkward. When this happens to you, as it undoubtedly will, try to understand what went wrong. If you don't understand why the sentence is awkward, discuss the sentence with your instructor. He will usually be able to identify the particular part of the sentence that he considers awkward, and he may be able to suggest other ways of phrasing the thought. Before going to your instructor, however, read the sentence carefully and write one or more alternative versions. If you are alert, you may discover the solution for yourself.

S 8 MIXED CONSTRUCTIONS

Sometimes you may carelessly shift from one type of construction to another in mid-sentence. Such errors can be caught by careful proofreading.

MIXED

When you have not prepared the assignment is embarrassing. (This sentence starts out well enough, but the dependent clause *When you have not prepared the assignment* unexpectedly becomes the subject of the verb *is*.)

REVISED

It is embarrassing to be asked a question in class when you are not prepared.

MIXED

Raising his arm to throw, a blitzing linebacker hit him.

REVISED

As the quarterback raised his arm to throw, a blitzing linebacker hit him.

or

Raising his arm to throw, the quarterback was jolted by a blitzing linebacker.

MIXED

The rain fell upon the tin roof amplified the sound.

REVISED

As the rain fell, the tin roof amplified the sound.

or

The tin roof amplified the sound of falling rain.

S 9 SHIFTS IN TENSE, PERSON, VOICE, OR MOOD

Avoid needless shifts in tense, person, voice, or mood.

SHIFT IN TENSE

As the pitcher *leaned* toward the plate, the catcher *gives* him the signal.
(There is a needless shift from past tense to present tense.)

REVISED

As the pitcher *leaned* toward the plate, the catcher *gave* him the signal.

SHIFT IN PERSON

If *you* use binoculars, *one* can sometimes see the signals from centerfield.
(There is a shift from second person to third person.)

REVISED

If *you* use binoculars, *you* can sometimes see the signals from centerfield.

If *one* uses binoculars, *he* can sometimes see the signals from centerfield.

SHIFT IN VOICE

As we *approached* the accident, a low groan *was heard*.
(There is a shift from active voice to passive voice.)

REVISED

As we *approached* the accident, we *heard* a low groan.

SHIFT IN MOOD

First *determine* the distance. Then you *should make* allowance for the wind.
(There is a shift from imperative mood to indicative mood.)

REVISED

First *determine* the distance. Then *make* allowance for the wind.

S 10 CONFUSING ELLIPTICAL CLAUSES

An elliptical clause with an implied subject may sometimes be misinterpreted. Avoid this problem by supplying the missing subject.

MISLEADING

When hit by flak and out of formation, the navigator

becomes one of the most important members of the crew.
(The navigator seems to have been hit by flak while flying out of formation.)

REVISED

When *a plane has been* hit by flak and *is* out of formation, the navigator becomes one of the most important members of the crew.

CONFUSING

Although alone in the car, the radio provided a link with the outside world.
(The radio seems to be alone in the car. Supply a clearly stated subject for the elliptical clause.)

REVISED

Although *he was* alone in the car, the radio provided a link with the outside world.

POSSIBLY CONFUSING

Once famous, the Beatles lost the simple joys of privacy.

REVISED

Once *they had become* famous, the Beatles lost the simple joys of privacy.

S 11 INVERSION

An inversion is the transposition of the normal order of the words in a sentence, such as placing the direct object or the verb before the subject.

NORMAL

I could not sleep.

INVERTED

Sleep I could not.

Sometimes, desirable effects of emphasis can be obtained by inversion, but more often than not inversion causes awkwardness. Use inversion rarely, if at all.

S 12 OMISSIONS

Do not carelessly omit necessary words.

CARELESS OMISSION

He said that a good salesman should know how to dress and approach a customer.

CORRECTED

He said that a good salesman should know how to dress and *how* to approach a customer.

CARELESS OMISSION

He stopped the traffic light.

CORRECTED

He stopped *for* the traffic light.

CARELESS OMISSION

He was tall, with black, curly hair and eyes.

CORRECTED

He was tall, with black, curly hair and *black* eyes.

OMISSION

I read the book had been published.
(Some readers might pause upon the combination "I read the book." Omission of *that* sometimes causes confusion, especially when the clause that it introduces follows a verb.)

CORRECTED

I read *that* the book had been published.

A FINAL EXAMPLE

An edition of the Bible printed in London in 1632 became known as the Wicked Bible because the printing omitted the word *not* in the Seventh Commandment, causing it to read: "Thou shalt commit adultery."

S 13 REPETITIOUS STRUCTURE OR PHRASING

Avoid the awkward repetition of subordinate constructions beginning with words like *who, which, that,* and *because.*

AWKWARD REPETITION

Because it was snowing, I did not go *because* of the hazardous driving conditions.

IMPROVED

I did not go because the snow had made driving hazardous.

Also avoid the awkward repetition of a word or variant of a word within the same sentence.

The *manufacturers* should *manufacture* more durable products.
(One of the italicized words should be changed.)

Our *players* all *played* well except for one unfortunate *play.*
(Find synonyms for two of the italicized words.)

S 14 SENTENCE LENGTH

Rewrite sentences that are too long. In the rewritten version, present the material in two or more sentences.

TOO LONG

Satire amuses by making its object appear ridiculous, but beneath the laughter it evokes is a serious criticism of human folly from the reference point of a standard of behavior which has been violated, and it cannot function without this norm of correct behavior, whether the norm is implied or directly stated.

IMPROVED

Satire amuses by making its object appear ridiculous, but beneath the ridicule is a serious criticism of human folly as a violation of a specific standard of behavior. Without this norm of correct behavior, whether implied or directly stated, satire cannot function.

Combine sentences that are too short, as in the sentences at the bottom of this page or the sentences in S 5.2.

See also S 6.2.

S 15 SENTENCE VARIETY

Vary the structure and length of your sentences. Avoid using too many short sentences or too many long ones in succession. Do not use the same sentence pattern repeatedly, unless you are using it for emphasis.

MONOTONOUS

Taylor bunted. The catcher raced for the ball. Taylor sprinted for first. The ball curved out of bounds.

This passage is monotonous, both in the number of short, choppy sentences and in the unvarying use of a subject-verb pattern at the beginning of each sentence.

IMPROVED

Taylor bunted and sprinted for first, but the ball veered out of bounds before the catcher could reach it.

Also see S 5.2.

Too many long sentences in succession can be just as monotonous as a series of short ones. After several long sentences, a short, incisive sentence provides an effective change of pace.

The following passage from Joan Didion's *Slouching Towards Bethlehem* contains only three sentences. Notice the variety in their construction and in their length, especially in the long first sentence and the short last one.

> The San Bernardino Valley lies only an hour east of Los Angeles by the San Bernardino Freeway but is in certain ways an alien place: not the coastal California of the subtropical twilights and the soft westerlies off the Pacific but a harsher California, haunted by the Mojave just beyond the mountains, devastated by the hot dry Santa Ana wind that comes down through the passes at 100 miles an hour and whines through the eucalyptus windbreaks and works on the nerves. October is the month for the wind, the month when breathing is difficult and the hills blaze up spontaneously. There has been no rain since April.

S 16 FALSE SUBJECT OR PREDICATE

The subject of a sentence, of course, names the thing which the sentence makes a statement about. The predication is what is said about the subject. It is essential that the relationship between the subject and the predicate be clear.

1. A false subject occurs when a subordinate idea is presented as the subject, while a potentially better subject is made subordinate.

FALSE SUBJECT

The frequency of commercials interrupts television programs.
(This statement is inaccurate since "frequency" does not interrupt. *Commercials* should be the subject, with the idea of frequency being conveyed by an adverb, *frequently.*)

REVISED

Commercials interrupt television programs frequently.

Or the sentence could be even more drastically rewritten, as follows:

Television programs are frequently interrupted by commercials.

2. A faulty predication occurs when the statement made about the subject is inappropriate, when it does not fit the subject.

FAULTY PREDICATE

His imagination was frightened by the thought of prison.
(Imagination cannot be frightened, although a person can. Either the subject or the predicate should be changed.)

REVISED

He was frightened by the thought of prison.

or

His imagination formed terrible visions of life in prison.

Clarity of Thought

C 1 AMBIGUITY

Be alert for distracting double meanings. In certain types of writing, you may deliberately exploit the ambiguities of language for ironic or humorous effects, but you do not want to produce unintended humor.

AMBIGUOUS

Legislators can't stop drinking.
(Who is drinking? The legislators?)

IMPROVED

Drinking can't be stopped by legislation.

or

Legislation can't stop drinking.

Sometimes you may mistakenly assume that what you have written corresponds to what you are thinking, whereas the words are actually only a vague approximation of your thought. The reader may be forced to guess at your meaning, and he may guess wrong.

Once the words have been written, you must be able to place yourself in the position of the reader, who cannot possibly share all of the connotative associations and assumptions that the words hold for you. Remember also that written language lacks the interpretive advantages of tone, emphasis, facial expression, and *ad hoc* explanation which a speaker is able to utilize. The reader will not necessarily read a passage as you would read it. Therefore, written language must be much clearer and more exact than spoken language.

When there is time, put your writing aside overnight and then try reading it critically and objectively, as though it were someone else's. If you are writing against time, you should still try to give your work a critical reading from the viewpoint of an imaginary reader. Such a reading will probably be effective to the extent that you can clearly picture your audience and vicariously identify with it.

C 2 COMPARISON

In making comparisons, be sure that the items are capable of being compared.

INCORRECT

His salary is larger than most college presidents.
(Comparison should be between similar items. A salary cannot be compared with a person, but it can be compared with another salary.)

CORRECT

His salary is larger than *that* of most college presidents.

C 3 DISTRACTING DETAILS

Do not overload your sentences with inconsequential details. If details distract the reader from the main idea or impression that you are trying to establish, they should be eliminated.

OVERLOADED WITH DISTRACTING DETAILS

The old house with a big tree in front of it on the corner of Oak and Franklin, which once belonged to my Uncle George, who went bankrupt in 1928 and moved to a small town in the eastern part of Texas to work in the oil fields (he's a millionaire now), is for sale.

IMPROVED

The old house on the corner of Oak and Franklin, which once belonged to my Uncle George, is for sale.

See S 6.2.

C 4 LOGICAL FALLACIES

Learn to detect the following logical fallacies.

1. Name calling (labeling). Discrediting someone's judgment or reliability by labeling him with a name that has unfavorable connotations.

DEROGATORY LABELS

Egghead, Extremist, Reactionary, Redneck, Fascist

Before using such labels, consider using a more precise and less emotionally biased word—e.g., "intellectual" instead of "egghead."

2. Argument *ad hominem*. An argument directed against the person with whom you disagree rather than against his ideas.

Smith's ideas about urban renewal may sound good, but, remember, he once served a prison term for income tax evasion.

The argument should be addressed to Smith's ideas, not to his personal history. His ideas on urban renewal should be judged only on their merits.

3. Transfer. The prestige or approval attached to one idea or person is transferred to another by association; for instance, a well-known movie star or athlete supports a certain political candidate. The prestige which the star has gained in one field of activity is transferred by association.

An expert's judgment in his field of special competence should be respected, but outside of his specialty he may be as subject to error and personal bias as the rest of us. A judgment on a particular subject should be respected in proportion to the knowledge, experience, and objectivity of the person making the judgment. Weigh these factors carefully before using or being influenced by the technique of transference.

4. Bandwagon. An attempt to persuade by an appeal to popular opinion.

> Everyone supports the war in Vietnam; therefore, it must be right.

Although majority opinion is to be respected, it is by no means infallible. Remember that for centuries men believed that the sun revolved around the earth. Don't let popular opinion prevent you from thinking for yourself. Consider the available evidence before forming an opinion.

5. Hasty generalization. A conclusion based on insufficient evidence.

> You are the second person that I have met today who has given up smoking. Cigarette sales must be declining.

The speaker's experience is too limited to support such a broad conclusion. On a national scale, cigarette sales may have actually increased.

6. *Post hoc, ergo propter hoc* (''After this; therefore, because of this''). Assuming a cause-and-effect relationship between two events simply because one follows the other.

> I went to a movie last night, and I made an *A* on the quiz this morning. From now on, I'm going to a movie before every quiz.

The student's assumption that going to a movie influenced his performance on the quiz is not necessarily a valid one. Too many other factors are involved.

7. Non sequitur ("It does not follow"). A conclusion not justified by the evidence or reasons given for it.

> John failed his driver's test; he must be stupid.

The conclusion is not justified by the evidence. John may simply have failed to study his driver's manual before taking the test. If so, he acted foolishly, but his failure does not prove that he is innately stupid.

8. Begging the question. Giving a conclusion (stated in slightly differing words) as a reason for a conclusion, or giving as proof a statement that itself is in need of proof or is based on an unproved assumption.

> Poems are not as exciting as novels because they are less interesting.
> (This is almost the same thing as saying that poems are less interesting than novels because they are less interesting. A slight variation on the statement is given as a reason for the statement.)
>
> Of course he is guilty. He was arrested, wasn't he?
> (The unproved assumption is that all people who are arrested are guilty.)

9. False dilemma. Unnecessarily limiting a choice to only two alternatives.

Young novelists today are influenced by either Hemingway or Faulkner.
(Actually, some young novelists are influenced by both; some are influenced by neither.)

10. False analogy. Analogies often help to explain how the speaker conceives of a subject, but they don't prove anything. When offered as logical proof, all analogies are "false." Use them as a means of indicating your attitude or explaining unfamiliar concepts, but do not think that you are *proving* anything when you use them.

The most efficient form of government is a dictatorship. After all, a team can't have eleven quarterbacks.
(The second statement clarifies the author's reason for making the first statement, but it by no means proves it. A football team and a government are not equivalents, despite some striking superficial resemblances.)

C 5 QUALIFICATION

Learn to qualify broad generalizations when they are not supported by known facts. Avoid absolute affirmations or negations unless they are clearly statements of personal opinion or unless you are deliberately overstating for emphasis or effect.

TOO BROAD

The death toll on our highways this year *will be* the highest in our history.

QUALIFIED

The death toll on our highways this year *may* (or *is expected to*) *be* the highest in our history.

TOO BROAD

No one makes an *A* in that course.

QUALIFIED

I have never known anyone who made an *A* in that course.

TOO BROAD

All freshmen like Salinger.

QUALIFIED

Many (or *some*, or *few*, as the case may be) freshmen like Salinger.

C 6 TRANSITION

Make sure that there is a smooth flow of thought between your sentences. If the transition from one sentence to another is abrupt or if the relationship is not clear, rephrase the sentences or insert an appropriate transitional word or phrase. (See *coherence*, p. 169.)

It is also important that the reader be able to see the relationship between paragraphs or between blocks of paragraphs. Whenever you shift from one aspect of your topic to another, be sure that the reader will be able to follow the turn of thought. Sometimes a transitional word or phrase, such as *nevertheless*, *on the other hand*, or *afterwards*, will be sufficient to signal a change to a different aspect of the subject. At other times a fuller explanation may be needed. Sometimes a whole paragraph may be used as a transition between segments of a paper.

> Buster Keaton was the other great comedian of the silent era. He rivaled Chaplin in his insights both into human nature and into the conflict between the individual man and the immense social machinery that surrounds him. Like Chaplin, he could make these insights both comic and serious at the same time. Van Hartmann

(After a long discussion of Charlie Chaplin in the preceding paragraphs, this short paragraph serves as a transition to

Buster Keaton, who becomes the subject of the next five paragraphs.)

Warning: As a general rule, use economy in your transitions. Don't overexplain what you intend to do and don't overload your sentences with transitional words or phrases. Too many words like *consequently* or phrases like *as a result* may impede the flow of thought and make your sentences difficult to read. Relatively simple transitions combined with a clear continuity of thought are more effective than too many obvious transitional words or phrases.

C 7 VAGUE GENERALITY

Phrase your generalizations as clearly as possible, and support them with facts, examples, or further explanations.

VAGUE

Fred is a great guy.

MORE SPECIFIC

I like Fred because he listens carefully to what I say and he doesn't become angry when we disagree.
(The reasons could be elaborated further, but this is enough to establish the idea that you need to state your meaning as specifically as possible—*great* is a blanket term of approval that could mean many things—and to give the reader at least some of the reasons for your generalization.)

VAGUE

The house was awful.

CLARIFIED BY DETAILS

The house was dilapidated. Paint was scaling from the walls.

The roof sagged, and a broken front window was mended with cardboard.

VAGUE

The movie was lousy.

MORE SPECIFIC

The movie began well, with the camera moving down the corridor of a prison, but it was soon evident that the director was more interested in violence for its own sake than he was in presenting an interesting story or believable characters. The violence soon became boring, and I left the theater in a state of depression.

Diction

D 1 METAPHORS AND MIXED METAPHORS

A metaphor is an assertion of similarity between two things not usually thought of as being similar. Sometimes the assertion is explicit (Love is madness); sometimes it is implicit (Jones *oozed* through the crowd).

A simile is simply a form of metaphor using *like* or *as* (Love is *like* madness).

Although the first example seems to state that love and madness are identical, it is saying only that in some ways love is similar to madness. Metaphors boldly overstate their case. They say, in effect, think of one thing (love) in terms of another (madness). They transcend the literal meaning of the statement. For instance, if you say, "Susan is a peach," you don't mean literally that Susan is a piece of fruit but that she is as pleasing to you as a delicious peach.

The metaphor in the sentence "Jones oozed through the crowd" is implied in the single word *ooze* rather than directly stated. Jones does not, of course, actually ooze through the crowd as oil oozes through a filter, but there is an implied similarity between the gradual but persistent nature of the two acts.

A good metaphor will produce a slight shock, a newness of perception. In a way, it transcends the usual meanings of words or the usual ways of looking at a thing. For instance, we all know that the word *dissect* means "to cut apart"; but when someone says, "She dissected me with a glance," it suddenly becomes a metaphor.

Since a minor jolt or newness of perception is essential in a good metaphor, metaphors that are used repeatedly over long periods of time lose their effectiveness; they become *clichés* (see D 3) or *dead metaphors*. Clichés are worn-out metaphors; dead metaphors are useful words that we are no longer aware of as metaphors (*honeymoon, disk jockey, black market*).

Metaphors can make your writing more vivid, and even add to its clarity, if they add fresh and genuine perceptions that ordinary language can't convey, but outworn or forced metaphors should be avoided. If an appropriate metaphor or simile does not come to mind naturally, simply state your idea in clear, concise English—with perhaps an example or a few vivid details to make it memorable.

FORCED METAPHOR

> The crashing glass played a light arpeggio upon the pavement, after the excruciating jazz of grinding metal and squealing rubber. Later a siren played a chilling solo.

The metaphors are so contrived that they distract the reader's attention from the action they are attempting to describe.

GROTESQUE SIMILE

> Her feet were like irregular mounds of unbaked dough, with small curved sausages attached at one end.

BETTER

> Her feet were short and broad, with a high arch and toes permanently distorted by a long succession of tight shoes.

When you are attempting to use metaphorical language, be careful not to cause confusion, or laughter, through a careless combination of metaphors.

MIXED METAPHOR

> My college courses are just a stepping stone to set off a fuse which will make me think.

(The two metaphors, "a stepping stone" and "a fuse," are awkwardly mixed. How can a stepping stone set off a fuse?)

D 2 NONSTANDARD WORDS

Avoid using words that are not used by educated writers or speakers. If in doubt about a particular word, consult your dictionary to see if it is listed or if the dictionary provides a label or comment on its usage.

NONSTANDARD

During the night one of our pipes *busted.*

REVISED

During the night one of our pipes *burst.*

NONSTANDARD

The announcer was *flustrated* by his inability to pronounce the word.

REVISED

The announcer was *frustrated* by his inability to pronounce the word.

The announcer was *flustered* by his inability to pronounce the word.

D 3 CLICHÉS

Clichés are stereotyped combinations of words, combinations that have been used so often and so automatically that they no longer evoke a fresh response. Familiar patterns can sometimes be useful (*in one sense, for the most part, as a consequence,* etc.), but stereotyped phrases that have been used too often have lost their ability to communicate, much like a joke or a record that you have heard too many times.

Ironically, the more original and effective a word is, the more likely it is to be dulled through overuse. The phrase "dead as a doornail," for instance, was once a very original expression, but it has been so overworked that we no longer perceive it vividly. It has become a cliché. Here is a brief list of clichés. You could easily think of others.

point with pride

a dull thud

view with alarm

burn the midnight oil

at one fell swoop

Clichés can sometimes be revitalized by a clever variation. The very fact that everyone knows what to expect from a cliché can increase the impact of a phrase that raises the expectation of a predictable combination but surprises the reader by breaking the pattern. This is what happens, for example, when an advertisement for a filter cigarette says, "Why settle for more?" (more nicotine, that is) rather than "Why settle for less?" Stereotyped phrases become detrimental to good writing, however, when they come to mind too automatically and are accepted too easily, giving the illusion of communicating but actually only signaling broad stereotyped responses. A good writer seeks a happy union of the familiar and the surprising. He may casually include a few easily recognized phrases now and then, if the occasion is informal and he feels that they will help him to establish an easy familiarity with his audience, but he will stop before he has used too many. He knows that writing which is too predictable is also dull.

D 4 DEADWOOD

Eliminate words that do not contribute significantly to the thought or connotation of a sentence. In all of the following examples, the words in italics could be eliminated without damage to the thought or connotation of the sentence.

> *In this modern world of* today we often hear of the dangers *inherent in the development* of automation.

Frequently a writer can express a thought more concisely by combining two sentences or by reducing clauses to phrases.

> *The car* ahead of us *was* a green Plymouth with Oregon license plates. *It* suddenly swerved into the lane of oncoming traffic.
>
> Suddenly *there was* a chilling hush *which* fell over the entire campus.

One well-chosen word is often more effective than a string of roughly synonymous ones:

> We watched with horror *and dismay* as the parachute continued to *plummet and* fall.

Redundance is a form of wordiness in which there is an unnecessary repetition of meaning.

> Endorse the check *on the back.*
>
> Please return the book *back* to its owner.
>
> The house was large *in size.*

D 5 GENERALIZED OR ABSTRACT DICTION

Your writing will be clearer and more interesting if you use specific nouns and verbs instead of general or abstract ones. When possible, use words that evoke vivid images or concrete sense impressions rather than vague generalities.

GENERALIZED

Jim bought a car.

MORE SPECIFIC

Jim bought a *frost-green 1970 Camaro.*

GENERALIZED

He *walked* down the street.

MORE SPECIFIC

Mr. Jones *waddled* down *Pennsylvania Avenue.*

GENERALIZED

He *ran* toward the goal.

MORE SPECIFIC

He *sprinted* (or perhaps *loped,* or *surged*) toward the goal.

ABSTRACT

Traffic *was impeded by adverse weather conditions.*

MORE CONCRETE

Traffic *inched along the ice-coated highway.*

D 6 IDIOMATIC USAGE

An **idiom** is a particular combination of words whose meaning has been established through usage. The combination is not always logical if one interprets each word literally, but a native speaker usually grasps the meaning easily because he is used to the combination as a unit without thinking of the meaning of individual words. A native speaker will not be troubled by common idioms such as "put up with," "come in handy," "pay off," or "go through with," but even native speakers may be doubtful about some combinations in formal writing—especially combinations involving verbs and prepositions, or nouns and prepositions. "In search for'' certainly makes as much sense as ''in search of,'' but the latter has been established by use as the correct idiom. When in doubt, consult a good dictionary or D 10 in this book.

D 7 JARGON

Jargon is specialized language used in a pretentious way or for an inappropriate audience. Usually it obscures rather than clarifies.

Any time you are trying to impress your reader by stating a relatively simple thought in an inflated style or by loading your writing with unnecessary technical terms, you are probably writing jargon. You can avoid jargon by thinking of your reader and by writing clearly so that he will understand.

Every field has its own technical vocabulary and therefore its own kind of potential jargon. The following sentence, with its technical terms and pretentious diction, is an example of literary jargon.

> This ironic persona of Donovan is further bifurcated into two cryptic analogues, George Dennis and Dennis George.
> (No one, not even the author, can be precisely sure of what this means.)

The term ''jargon'' may be extended to include any passage of pretentious, overblown diction.

> JARGON
>
> The organic crimson-tinted clouds swept over the ominous slashes of the sunset sea, looming, portentous—finally weeping their crucified sorrows upon us, wrapping the shore in a dark enigmatic mantle.
>
> CLEARER
>
> The sky darkened as the clouds swept across the sea toward us. Then the rain began, obscuring the shoreline.

D 8 CONNOTATION

Connotation is the associative nuances of a word or phrase, rather than its literal meaning (**denotation**). The literal or denotative meaning of *mother,* for instance, is "female parent," but the connotative attitudes produced in the readers might range from sentimental approval to repugnance, although in our society most of the associations would be favorable. Some words tend to be strongly connotative, whether favorably (*mother*) or unfavorably (*murderer*); other words are relatively neutral (*way, example, unit*). But words are also influenced by their context. For instance, in the following combinations the connotative associations of the nouns are modulated by the adjectives: a *nagging* mother, a *condemned* murderer, a *dark* way. In more extensive combinations of words (say, throughout a paragraph or a lyric poem), the connotative interactions can be extremely subtle and complex.

As a general rule, it is better to use a few strongly connotative words carefully than it is to use too many. A sentence that is overloaded with highly connotative words will seem too high pitched and emotional, or too sentimental. See, for instance, the final example in D 7.

D 9 VARIETIES OF USAGE

Your choice of words will vary as you shift from one kind of writing to another, or from one audience to another—just as it does when you are speaking to different people in different situations. You would not, for instance, speak in the same way in a bull session with friends as you would in a job interview or in a public address. Nor would you use the kinds of words in a short informal essay that you would use in a long research paper. Even the language of your letters will vary as you write to different people—to your parents, for example, or to a newspaper editor, or to a friend.

One way to talk about variations in usage is in terms of dialects. A **dialect** is a pattern of linguistic usage shared by a special group, whether it is based on a common regional background, on mutual social, ethnic, or professional experience, on age, or even on sex. People who use the same dialect share a common set of linguistic patterns that differ from the more general usage of standard English. When you are dealing with a small and known audience—a particular friend, for instance—you have no trouble in adjusting to the proper dialect. But as your audience becomes larger and less clearly defined, a single dialect or even a mix of one or two dialects will no longer suffice, and you will have to shift to more inclusive patterns. The general pattern of appropriate usage for all literate writers is called **standard English.**

Standard English, however, may be more formal or less formal according to the purpose and occasion for which it is being used. A great deal depends on the writer's estimation of his audience and of what the occasion calls for. Not only does he have to calculate the dialect, or lack of it, that would be most appropriate for his audience, he also has to consider the degree of formality that would be appropriate for the type of paper that he is writing. An essay based on personal experience may seem stilted if the language is too impersonal and formal; on the other hand, a reader may find colloquial language or slang distracting in a paper where a greater degree of formality is expected.

Most dictionaries indicate words which vary from standard usage by providing labels such as *slang, archaic, dialect,* and so on. Although usage labels can make you aware that certain words are not ordinarily used in standard English (see *ain't, crap, tote, rap,* for instance), checking the dictionary for labels can be rather cumbersome when you are in a hurry, and it is not always easy to interpret such labels in regard to a particular writing situation. Also, since dictionaries are always behind actual usage, some slang words or neologisms may not even be in the dictionary, or, if they are, the definitions may be outdated. Usage labels are helpful up to a point, but they will not cover every situation. Use them when they seem helpful, but try to develop your own sense of the appropriate kinds of words for each assignment. Ask yourself what dialect (including standard English) or what degree of formality would be most effective for the occasion. In making your choice, consider your audience, the kind of response you want, and the type of paper you are writing.

As a general rule, when you are in doubt, you should probably incline toward standard English. But don't play it safe all the time. Merely safe or correct writing can be very dull. Colloquial or informal English can make your writing livelier and more familiar, but it should be used with an awareness of the context in which you are writing. Don't mix different kinds of usage in a haphazard or jarring manner. Don't, for instance, shift from formal English to slang or from standard English to a dialect unless you have a good reason for doing so. If you do make sudden shifts in diction, try to incorporate them within a generally consistent context. If your paper is to have a unified tone, one type of diction should predominate.

D 10 WORD CHOICE

Sometimes you may jot down a word that only approximates your meaning, or even distorts it. Or you may choose a word that is not appropriate for the context in which you have used it. The best way to avoid such errors is to proofread carefully and, when in doubt, to consult a dictionary. For quick reference, words that are frequently confused or misused are listed below, in alphabetical order.

A, an. *A* is used before a consonant sound or the sound of *y* or *w*.

A car, *a* hospital, *a* university, *a* one-way street

An is used before a vowel or a silent *h.*

An egg, *an* hour

Accept, except. *Accept* (verb) means *to receive. Except* (verb) means *to exclude. Except* (preposition) means *but.*

Jonas was accused of *accepting* a bribe.

We *excepted* him from the list of candidates.

We invited all of the class members *except* John.

Adapt, adopt. *Adapt* means *to modify* or *adjust. Adopt* means *to choose.*

Dinosaurs became extinct because they were unable to *adapt* themselves to a changing environment.

The selection committee has *adopted* a new textbook for next year.

Advice, advise. *Advise* is a verb; *advice* is a noun.

He *advised* me to write at least one paragraph every day. I followed his *advice.*

Affect, effect. *Affect* (verb) means *to influence. Effect* (verb) means *to cause, bring about. Effect* (noun) means *a result.*

Economic factors will greatly *affect* the November elections.

He hopes to *effect* a change in company policy.

His speech did not produce the desired *effect.*

Aggravate. In formal writing *aggravate* means *to intensify* or *make worse.* It is sometimes used colloquially, however, to mean *to irritate* or *annoy.*

FORMAL

The salty nuts *aggravated* my thirst.

COLLOQUIAL

His continual complaining *aggravated* me.

Agree to, with. One agrees *to* a plan, but *with* a person. I agreed *to* John's proposal. I agreed *with* John.

Allude, elude. *Allude* means *to refer indirectly. Elude* means *to evade, escape.*

He *alluded* to Hemingway's death.

He *eluded* all attempts to capture him.

Allusion, illusion. An *allusion* is an *indirect reference.* An *illusion* is a *false impression.*

Paradise Lost is full of biblical *allusions.*

A mirage is an *illusion.*

All ready. An incorrect spelling of the adverb *already.*

When we arrived, the game had *already* started.
(*All ready* is correct, however, in constructions such as "We were *all ready* to go.")

Alot. Written as two words (*a lot*) and not used in formal writing.

Alright. An incorrect spelling of *all right.*

Altar, alter. An *altar* (noun) is a place for the performance of religious rites. *Alter* (verb) means *to change.*

The priest turned and faced the *altar.*

He decided to *alter* his plans.

All together. An incorrect spelling of the adverb *altogether*.

He missed the target *altogether*.
(*All together* is correct, however, in constructions such as "After many years of separation, we were all together.")

Among, between. *Between* usually refers to only two, *among* to more than two.

She stood *between* John and Henry.

She divided the cake *among* the three children.

Amount, number. *Amount* refers to things in mass. *Number* refers to countable objects.

He sold a large *amount* of gas.

He sold a large *number* of cars.

An. See *A*.

And etc. Omit *and*.

Ante-, anti-. *Ante* means *before*. *Anti* means *against*.

*Ante*bellum, *anti*freeze

Apt. See *Likely*.

As, as if, like. See *Like*.

Ascent, assent. *Ascent* (noun) means *the act of ascending* or *rising*. *Assent* (verb) means *to agree to*. *Assent* (noun) means *agreement, approval*.

We watched the slow *ascent* of the rocket as it gradually gained momentum.

The mayor *assented* to the committee's proposal.

Reluctantly, the mayor gave his *assent*.

Awful, awfully. *Awful,* literally, means *full of awe, inspiring awe*. It should not be used in formal writing as an indefinite term of disapproval or as a substitute for *very* or *extremely*.

FORMAL

The report was *inaccurate* (or *tedious* perhaps, but not *awful*).

FORMAL

I am *very* (not *awful* or *awfully*) tired.

Bad, badly. The adjective *bad,* not the adverb *badly,* is used after a linking verb.

I feel *bad*.

The coffee tastes *bad*.

Bare, bear. *Bare* means *naked, uncovered*. *Bear* means *carry, endure,* or an animal, such as a grizzly bear.

Between. See *Among*.

Break, brake. Do not confuse these two homonyms. A *brake* is a device for slowing or stopping a machine or vehicle.

As I approached the intersection, I applied the *brakes,* but the car continued to slide on the ice.

Bust, busted, bursted. Nonstandard for *burst*.

During the cold weather the water pipe *burst*.

But that, but what, but. Do not use for *that* after the verb *doubt*.

I do not doubt *that* (not *but that, but what,* or *but*) he will succeed.

But. Do not use *but* with a negative when it means *only*.

DOUBLE NEGATIVE

I *don't* have *but* one friend left.

REVISED

I have *but* (or *only*) one friend left.

Can, may. In colloquial usage either of these is used to request permission. In a formal situation, when you want to express politeness, use *may*.

May I sit here?

Can't hardly. Colloquial. Don't use *hardly* with a negative in formal writing.

COLLOQUIAL

I *can't hardly* see.

FORMAL

I can *hardly* see.

Can't help but. Colloquial, not to be used in formal writing.

COLLOQUIAL

I *can't help but* admire him.

FORMAL

I *can't help* admiring him.

Capital, capitol. The *capital* is the city in which the *capitol* (building) is located.

Raleigh is the *capital* of North Carolina.

The *capitol* is located in Raleigh.

Center around. It is impossible to center *around* something. Use center *on*.

Choose, chose. *Choose* is present tense. *Chose* is past tense.

Cite, sight, site. *Cite* means to *refer to, quote,* or *summon*. *Sight* means *a thing seen*. A *site* is *a location for a building*.

He *cited* statistics on traffic fatalities.

After the trip, home was a welcome *sight*.

He purchased a building *site*.

Compatible *with*.

Complement, compliment. *Complement* means *that which completes*. *Compliment* means *an expression of praise or admiration*. The same basic distinction exists between *complementary* and *complimentary,* and between *complement* (verb) and *compliment* (verb).

A good defense *complements* (supplements) a good offense.

A wise man occasionally *compliments* (praises) his wife.

Conscience, conscious. *Conscience* (a noun) means *an individual's sense of right and wrong*. *Conscious* (an adjective) means *aware*.

Smith has a troubled *conscience*.

Although severely injured, John remained *conscious*.

Continual, continuous. *Continual* means *recurring steadily at intervals*. *Continuous* means *occurring without interruption*.

He was awakened by the *continual* ringing of the telephone.

He watched the slow, *continuous* flow of the river.

Could of. Incorrect for *could have.*

Council, counsel. A *council* is an administrative group or assembly. *Counsel* (noun) means *advice* or *advisor. Counsel* (verb) means to *give advice.*

He is a member of the Honor *Council.*

Mr. Smith gave me good *counsel* last semester.

He *counseled* me to change my major.

Credible, credulous. *Credible* means *worthy of belief* (said of an assertion). *Credulous* means *believing too readily* (said of a person).

His story was not *credible.*

John is too *credulous;* he believes the television commercials.

Criteria, criterion. *Criteria* is the plural of *criterion.*

What are your *criteria* for success?
(The question implies more than one criterion.)

His chief *criterion* is money.

Data. The plural of *datum.* The singular *datum* is seldom used. Some writers now use *data* for both the singular and the plural.

These *data* are extremely important.

Differ from, differ with. *Differ from* means *to be unlike in some respect. Differ with* means *to disagree.*

My musical preferences *differ from* yours.

I *differ with* you on that subject.

Different than. *Different from* is the preferred form, although *different than* is used colloquially.

Jane is certainly *different from* her mother.

The university is *different from* what I had expected.

Disinterested. Means *impartial.* Do not use it as a synonym for *uninterested.*

To be effective, a mediator must be *disinterested.*

Doing, during. *Doing* is used as a part of a verb phrase or as a verbal. *During* is a preposition that specifies a time relationship.

Greta is *doing* her homework.

Millions of people were killed *during* World War II.

Dove. Colloquial for *dived.*

He *dived* (not *dove*) into the pool.

Dual, duel. *Dual* means *double. Duel* means *a formal fight with deadly weapons.*

His car has *dual* exhausts.

He challenged his rival to a *duel.*

Due to. Many people object to the use of *due to* to introduce an adverbial phrase, as in this sentence: *Due to* his carelessness, two people were injured.

PREFERABLE

Because of his carelessness, two people were injured.

No one objects to the use of *due* as a predicate adjective.

CORRECT

His low grades were *due to* his poor attendance.

Effect. See *Affect.*

Elicit, illicit. *Elicit* means to *draw forth, evoke. Illicit* means *illegal.*

The district attorney tried to *elicit* a confession from the suspect.

The police believed that he was engaged in the *illicit* sale of drugs.

Elude. See *Allude.*

Emigrate, immigrate. *Emigrate* means *to move from a country. Immigrate* means *to move to a country.*

Eminent, imminent. *Eminent* means *prominent. Imminent* means *impending, about to occur.*

He is an *eminent* physician.

Rain was *imminent.*

Except. See *Accept.*

Explicit, implicit. *Explicit* means *clearly and specifically stated. Implicit* means *implied* or *understood without being actually stated.*

His words were very *explicit,* but his actions were an *implicit* denial of what he was saying.

Fewer, less. *Fewer* refers to countable quantities (*fewer* cars, *fewer* students, *fewer* errors). *Less* refers to noncountable quantities or abstractions (*less* sugar, *less* expensive, *less* frequent, *less* important). *Fewer* cannot be used as a substitute for *less* (you would not, for instance, say "fewer sugar"), but *less* is used fairly often in place of *fewer:* "There are *fewer* (or *less*) cars on campus this year." Some people, however, object to the use of *less* as a substitute for *fewer*. If you think some of your readers might be distracted or annoyed by the use of *less* for *fewer,* then maintain the distinction cited by the rule above.

Good. Do not use as an adverb in formal writing.

> COLLOQUIAL
>
> He plays *good.*
>
> FORMAL
>
> He plays *well.*

But after linking verbs (*sounds, seems, tastes, is, looks,* etc.) the adjective form *good* is correct.

> The rain in the pines sounds *good.*
>
> The coffee tastes *good.*
>
> Sue looks *good* in a bathing suit.

Good and. Colloquial for *very.*

> COLLOQUIAL
>
> He was *good and* tired.
>
> FORMAL
>
> He was *very* tired.

Great. Do not use as a general term of approval, as in "He was a great guy." Try to be more specific. See C 7.

Had of. Incorrect for *had*.

INCORRECT

I wish I *had of* gone.

CORRECT

I wish I *had* gone.

Hanged, hung. Use *hanged* when referring to an execution; otherwise, use *hung*.

Only one woman has been *hanged* in this state.

The picture was *hung* unevenly.

Hardly. Has the effect of a negative. Do not use with *not*.

COLLOQUIAL

I *can't hardly* believe it.

FORMAL

I *can hardly* believe it.

Hopefully. This word is frequently used colloquially to mean "I hope," "we hope," "it is to be hoped that."

Hopefully, I will graduate.

Hopefully, the war will end soon.

Many people, however, object to this usage, maintaining that hopefully should be used only as an adverb meaning "in a hopeful manner."

The hitchhiker looked *hopefully* at the approaching car.

Illicit. See *Elicit*.

Illusion. See *Allusion*.

Immigrate. See *Emigrate*.

Imminent. See *Eminent*.

Implicit. See *Explicit*.

Imply, infer. *Imply* means to *hint* or *suggest*. *Infer* means to *draw a conclusion* or *make an assumption*. A writer or speaker *implies;* a reader, listener, or observer *infers*.

> The candidate *implied* that his opponent was a communist sympathizer.
>
> After looking at birth rates for the last twenty years, he *inferred* that there would be a decline in college enrollments.

In, into. *In* means *within*. *Into* indicates motion from outside to inside.

> When I arrived he was waiting *in* his office.
>
> He hurried *into* his office.

Incredible, incredulous. *Incredible* means *not worthy of belief* (said of an assertion or action). *Incredulous* means *unwilling to believe, expressing strong doubt* (said of a person).

> Tom told us an *incredible* story.
>
> We exchanged *incredulous* looks.

Infer. See *Imply*.

Ingenious, ingenuous. *Ingenious* means *clever, resourceful*. *Ingenuous* means *frank, innocent, without guile*.

> He had an *ingenious* ability to produce inventions that seemed amazingly simple, once he had thought of them.

She looked at him with an *ingenuous* smile.

In search *of*.

Irregardless. Incorrect for *regardless*.

Is because, is where, is when. Many people object to these constructions. In formal writing, avoid them when another construction will serve just as effectively.

Its, it's. *Its* is the possessive of *it*. *It's* is an abbreviation of *it is*.

Kind of. Colloquial for *somewhat* or *rather*.

The question was *somewhat* (not *kind of*) confusing.

Laid, lain. *Laid* is the past tense and past participle of *lay* (meaning to *put* or *place*). *Lain* is the past participle of *lie* (meaning *to recline*). *Laid* always has a direct object. *Lain* never has a direct object. See *Lay, lie*.

Later, latter. Do not confuse *later*, which means *at a later time*, with *latter*, which means *the second of two previously mentioned things*.

I will see you *later*.

Football seems to have replaced baseball as our nation's favorite sport, but I still prefer the *latter*.

Lay, lie. *Lay* (meaning to *place* or *put*) always has a direct object. *Lie* (meaning to *recline*) never has a direct object.

Lie down and rest.

Lay the book on the table.

The principal parts of *lie* are *lie, lay, lain.*
The principal parts of *lay* are *lay, laid, laid.*
Notice that the past tense of *lie* and the present tense of *lay* are spelled alike.

> Yesterday I *lay* in the sun for an hour.
>
> Please *lay* the book on the table.

Lead, led. The past tense (and past participle) of the verb *lead* is *led.*

> He *led* the league in home runs.
>
> His hitting *has led* the team to several crucial victories.

Learn. Incorrect for *teach.*

> She agreed to *teach* (not *learn*) him how to type.

Leave, let. Do not confuse *leave* (to *go away from, allow to remain*) with *let* (to *permit*).

> *Let* (not *leave*) me do it.
>
> *Leave* the door open.
>
> *Let* (not *leave*) the door stay open.

Leave and *let* are interchangeable in the following idiom: *Leave* (or *let*) me alone.

Less. See *Fewer.*

Liable. See *Likely.*

Lie. See *Lay.*

Like. Do not use *like* to introduce a dependent clause. Instead, use *as, as if,* or *as though.*

He acts *as if* (not *like*) he knows what he is doing.

Likely, liable, apt. Do not confuse *likely* (suggesting probability) with *liable* (meaning *subject to*) or *apt* (meaning *inclined, suitable,* or *proficient*).

Accidents are *likely* to happen to a careless driver.

A careless driver is *liable* to accidents.

He is *apt* (or *likely,* but not *liable*) to be rude.

He made an *apt* comment.

He is an *apt* student.

Literally. This means "exactly," "actually," "precisely as stated." Do not use it loosely as an intensifier, as in this sentence: Our fullback is *literally* a Sherman tank. (This would be unfair competition, unless the opposing team were allowed a bulldozer.)

Loose, lose. Do not confuse *loose* (to *free from restraint, unconfined, not dense*) with *lose* (to *fail to keep, suffer defeat*).

One may *lose* (not *loose*) a battle and still win the war.

Lot of. Do not use in formal writing for *much* or *many.*

Many (not *a lot of*) accidents could be avoided.

Maybe, may be. The word *maybe* is an adverb. The words *may be* serve as part of a verb phrase. Do not confuse the spelling of the two.

Maybe the store will be closed tonight.

The store *may be* closed tonight.

May of. Incorrect for *may have.*

Media. The plural of *medium*, as in the phrase *the mass media*.

Might of. Incorrect for *might have*.

Moral, morale. Do not confuse *moral* (meaning *pertaining to a distinction between right and wrong*) with *morale* (meaning *mental attitude*).

> The court's decision was both *moral* and just.
>
> The *morale* of the team was good.

Most. Colloquial for *almost*.

> *Almost* (not *most*) everyone thought that he would win.

Must of. Incorrect for *must have*.

Myself, yourself, himself. Do not use intensive and reflexive pronouns as personal pronouns.

> She smiled at Tom and me (not *at Tom and myself*).

Nice. Overused as a word of general approval. Seek a more specific word.

Not . . . no, not . . . nothing. Some readers insist that two negatives cancel each other and that a statement such as "I will not buy nothing" means "I will buy something." In formal writing, do not use two negatives unless you are deliberately using them to make a positive statement.

> DOUBLE NEGATIVE
>
> I will *not* concede *nothing*.
> (Some people would read this as an emphatic denial. Others would interpret it to mean "I will concede something.")

FORMAL

I will *not* concede *anything*.

or

I will concede *nothing*.

Noted, notorious. Both *noted* and *notorious* mean *widely known*, but *noted* has favorable connotations whereas *notorious* has unfavorable connotations.

He is a *noted* physicist.

He is a *notorious* criminal.

Nowadays. Do not use. Simply say *now* or *today*.

Nowhere near. Colloquial for *not nearly*.

There was *not nearly* (not *nowhere near*) enough food for all of us.

Number. See *Amount*.

Off of. *Of* is unnecessary.

He fell *off* (not *off of*) the fence.

OK, o.k., okay. Do not use in formal writing.

On account of. Do not use to introduce a dependent clause.

He was absent *because* (not *on account of*) he was ill.

Ought to of. Incorrect for *ought to have*.

Over with. Colloquial for *finished, over*.

The game was *over* (not *over with*).

Part *with* (a thing), *from* (a person).

Party. Incorrect for *person* or *individual.*

Pastime. Frequently misspelled as *pass time.*

Personal, personnel. Do not confuse the adjective *personal* (meaning *peculiar to a certain person*) with the noun *personnel* (meaning *persons employed in a certain job*).

> He resigned for *personal* reasons.
>
> The comptroller was pleased with the *personnel* working under him.

Phenomenon, phenomena. *Phenomenon* is singular. *Phenomena* is plural.

> The recent popularity of science fiction is an interesting *phenomenon* (not *phenomena*).

Plan on. Colloquial for *plan to.*

Plus. Don't use this word as a conjunction.

Precede, proceed. *Precede* means *to go before. Proceed* means *to go on, to continue in an orderly manner.* The phrase *proceed to* is often deadwood in a sentence and generally should be avoided.

> WORDY
>
> After sitting at the desk, he *proceeded to sharpen* (instead of the more concise *sharpened*) six lead pencils.

Predominate. Like its root word, *dominate,* this is a verb. Don't use it as an adjective.

INCORRECT

The *predominate* winds are from the south.

CORRECT

The *predominant* winds are from the south.

Pretty. This is colloquial for *fairly, very,* or *almost.*

COLLOQUIAL

I was *pretty* sure that I was right.

FORMAL

I was *confident* that I was right.

or

I was *almost* certain that I was right.

Principal, principle. *Principal* (adjective) means *chief* or *foremost. Principle* (noun) means *a general law* or *rule. Principal* (noun) means *a sum of money which draws interest* or *the chief official of a school.*

The Mississippi is our *principal* river.

He believes in the *principle* of self-determination.

He managed to live on the interest from his *principal.*

The *principal* spoke cordially to the new teacher.

Prophecy, prophesy. *Prophecy* is a noun. *Prophesy* is a verb. See your dictionary for the difference in pronunciation.

He *prophesied* the end of the world, but his *prophecy* did not come true.

Quiet, quite. Do not confuse *quiet* (*calm, not noisy*) with *quite* (*completely, entirely*).

He is a *quiet* man.

I do not *quite* agree with you.

He was *quite* angry.

Real. An adjective, not an adverb. Do not use for *very* or *extremely.*

He was *very* (not *real*) hungry.

Respectively, respectfully. *Respectively* means *in the order named. Respectfully* means *with respect.*

The guitar and the banjo belong to John and George *respectively.*

Respectfully (not *respectively*) yours . . .

Rise, raise. *Rise (rose, risen)* means *to get up, ascend. Raise (raised, raised)* means *to lift, cause to rise. Raise* always has a direct object; *rise* never has a direct object.

The flag *rose* slowly.

He *raised* the flag.

See where. Do not use this phrase when you mean *see that* or *read that.*

I see in the paper *that* (not *where*) the Smiths have a new baby.

Should of. Incorrect for *should have.*

Sight, site. See *Cite.*

Sit, set. *Sit (sat, sat)* means to *sit down. Set (set, set)* means to *put* or *place. Sit* never has a direct object. *Set* always has a direct object.

Please *sit* down.

Set the vase by the window.

So. Do not use as an intensive.

COLLOQUIAL

He is *so* clever.

FORMAL

He is *very* clever.

So that. *So that* is preferable to *so* in introducing clauses.

We posted our land *so that* we would not be bothered by trespassers.

Sort of. Colloquial. In formal writing, *somewhat* or *rather* is preferred.

He was *somewhat* (not *sort of*) tired.

Stationary, stationery. *Stationary* is an adjective meaning *in a fixed position, unmoving*. *Stationery* is a noun meaning *paper used for writing*.

Statue, stature, statute. A *statue* is a sculptured figure. *Stature* refers to height or size. A *statute* is a law.

The *statue* slowly toppled from its pedestal.

Their fullback has the *stature* of a Sherman tank.

Many old *statutes* are no longer enforced.

Such. Do not use as an intensifier in formal writing.

COLLOQUIAL

He is *such* an interesting person!

FORMAL

He is a *very* interesting person.

Sure. An adjective. Do not use for *surely* or *certainly.*

I *surely* (not *sure*) am tired.

Sure and. Colloquial for *sure to.*

Be *sure to* (not *sure and*) drive carefully.

Teach. See *Learn.*

Than, then. *Than* is a function word used for comparisons. *Then* is an adverb indicating the time of an action.

He stayed longer *than* he had intended.

He aimed the rifle carefully; *then* he squeezed the trigger.

Their, there, they're. *Their* is a possessive adjective. *There* is an adverb or expletive. *They're* is a contraction of the verb phrase *they are.*

I do not know *their* address.

Have you ever been *there?*

There are several solutions to that problem.

They're leaving early.

These kind, those kind. Be sure that a noun modified by *this* or *that* is singular and that a noun modified by *these* or *those* is plural.

this kind, *that* kind

these kinds, *those* kinds

Thusly. Use *thus.*

To, too, two. Do not confuse the preposition *to* (*to* class, *to* the car) with the adverb *too* (*too* hot) or the number *two* (one, *two,* three).

Try and. Colloquial for *try to.*

Unique. Means *the only one of its kind.* Not to be modified by *more, most, very,* etc.

Use to. Colloquial. Should be written *used to.*

Which, who, that, whose. *Which* refers to things. *Who* refers to persons. *That* and *whose* may refer to persons or things.

While. Overused as a substitute for *although* or *whereas. While* is usually thought of as referring to time.

Whose, who's. *Whose* is the possessive form of the pronoun *who. Who's* is a contraction of *who is.*

> She is a person *whose* opinion I respect.
>
> *Who's* going to win?

Worse, worst. Do not confuse the comparative form *worse* (for comparing two things) with the superlative form *worst* (for comparing more than two things).

> Your pun is *worse* than mine.
>
> That is the *worst* pun I have ever heard.

Would. *Would* is frequently misused by writers who are trying to indicate that a hypothetical, conditional, or desired action did not actually happen. Constructions like the following are especially troublesome.

INCORRECT

If I *would have* known you were selling tickets, I would have bought one.

CORRECT

If I *had* known you were selling tickets, I would have bought one.

INCORRECT

I wished that I *would have* gone.

CORRECT

I wished that I *had* gone.

See G 7.3, p. 30.

Would of. Incorrect for *would have*.

Your, you're. *Your* is a possessive pronoun. *You're* is a contraction of the verb phrase *you are*. One cannot be used for the other.

You're going back to *your* house already?

Yourself. See *Myself*.

Punctuation

Pu 1 APOSTROPHE

An apostrophe is used

1. To indicate the possessive case of nouns and of some indefinite pronouns.

A man's work, children's games, Mr. Jones' car, Kurtz's last words, everyone's opinion

See G 4.3, p. 12.

2. To indicate omission of letters and numbers (not to be used in formal writing).

don't, I'm, he's (contractions of *do not, I am, he is*)

the class of '72 (1972)

3. To form plurals of numbers, letters, and words.

There are two *3's* in your telephone number.

Be sure to dot your *i's*.

How many *and's* are in that sentence?

Pu 2 BRACKETS

Brackets are used within a quotation to set off material inserted by another writer.

"On his deathbed, Herbert sent the manuscript of *The*

Temple to his friend [Nicholas Farrar] at Little Gidding.'' (The name of the friend is inserted by a later writer for the reader's information.)

''Milton's widow recieved [*sic*] eight pounds for all her rights to the second edition of *Paradise Lost*.''
(The word *sic*—Latin for *thus*—is inserted by the person quoting this passage to indicate that he is not responsible for the misspelling of *received.* It was thus in the original.)

Pu 3 COLON

A colon is used

1. After introductory statements. The words following the colon usually elaborate or explain more fully the statement preceding the colon.

Tonight I would like to discuss a poet much admired but seldom read: Whitman.

He has a full schedule: chemistry, Latin, calculus, and a blonde named Mary.

One thing is certain: the crisis is near.

The reasons for the accident were obvious: (1) The driver of the Volkswagen was intoxicated. (2) He was traveling east at sixty miles per hour. (3) Merritt Avenue is a one-way street with traffic flowing west.

Note: As a general rule, colons are used only after complete statements.

NO COLON REQUIRED

The causes for this unrest are low pay, poor working

conditions, and lack of communication between labor and management.

COLON NEEDED

There are three causes for this unrest: low pay, poor working conditions, and lack of communication between labor and management.

(Notice, however, the colon after ''Note'' below.)

Note: The first word following a colon is not usually capitalized unless it is a proper noun, the first word of a quotation, or the first word in a series of sentences introduced by the material preceding the colon. See the examples given above.

2. **To introduce quotations.** See Pu 18.6 and Pu 20.

3. **After the salutation of a formal letter.**

Dear Sir:

4. **After the chapter number of a Biblical reference.**

Judges 13:1

5. **After the hour in a reference to hours and minutes.**

10:15 a.m.

6. **As a means of emphasizing the words following the colon.**

There is only one person whom he admires without reservation: himself.

The thought of this sentence might have been stated in another manner, but not without losing the ironic emphasis on *himself* which the colon provides.

Pu 4 COMMA

Commas are used

1. To separate two independent clauses joined by a coordinate conjunction (*and, but, or*), unless the clauses are very short.

The long line inched forward with intolerable slowness, and a cold wind numbed our faces.

2. To separate words, phrases, or clauses in a series.

Gaskin maneuvered through a maze of glasses, trays, and elbows.

The dust seeped under the window sills, across the room, and into the food.

She knew what he liked, what he merely tolerated, and what he abhorred.

3. To set off introductory verbal phrases.

Bursting into the room, he confronted two startled faces.

To begin the morning, he sorted a large stack of letters.

After evading the last tackler, he raced toward the goal.

4. To set off introductory dependent clauses.

After he had evaded the last tackler, he tripped and fell.

5. To set off nonrestrictive phrases and clauses.

Smith, a politician, strode purposefully toward the booth.

Mays, sensing an opportunity, sprinted toward second.

The catcher, who was usually accurate, threw the ball over the shortstop's head.

6. To set off concluding clauses and phrases. (This punctuation is often optional.)

A line was already forming, although the tickets would not go on sale until the next morning.

I was comfortably warm in my sleeping bag, despite the falling snow.

Carew is a menacing batter, especially with men on base.

(In the sentences above, the commas are appropriate, since the comments following the commas provide additional but nonrestrictive information. Frequently, however, the commas are optional, depending upon the closeness of the relationship between the parts of the sentence or upon whether or not a slight pause is desired.)

He left early because he wanted to avoid the postgame traffic.

(A comma could be used after *early* if the writer wanted a slight pause at that point, but it is not necessary. In fact, in this case it would probably be better not to use one.)

Fisher won the match because his opponent was unable to concentrate.

(Because both clauses seem necessary for the full meaning, the comma should be omitted in this sentence.)

7. To separate coordinate adjectives (adjectives that equally modify the same word).

His only reaction was a *fleeting, tentative* smile.

Note: When the order of the adjectives is optional (*a fleeting, tentative smile* or *a tentative, fleeting smile*), the adjectives are separated from each other by a comma. But when the order of the adjectives is fixed by idiomatic usage (*a small dining room*), the adjectives are not separated by a comma.

8. To separate items in dates.

On December 7, 1941, the Japanese attacked Pearl Harbor.

9. To separate items in addresses and geographical references.

Until recently, 118 West Tryon Street, Hillsborough, North Carolina, was known simply as the Nash-Hooper House.

10. To introduce quotations. See Pu 18.6.

11. To conclude the salutation of an informal letter.

Dear John,

12. To set off transitional words and phrases.

I realize, however, that my evidence is far from complete.

In other words, that policy would be disastrous.

13. To prevent misreading.

Inside, Professor Smith was reading the evening paper.

By the end of line forty, one realizes that the poem is a satire.

(Try reading these sentences without the commas.)

14. To set off interruptions in direct quotations.

''Spring is the time,'' he said, ''when I become restless.''

Note: If the interrupting phrase is inserted at a point in the quotation where a mark of punctuation stronger than a comma would be required, then that mark of punctuation is placed after the interrupting phrase.

“Science fiction is interesting,” he said. “It has a way of becoming history.”

Notice these slight variants:

“Are you going?” she asked. “It should be an interesting party.”

“I’m leaving!” he shrieked. “No one can stop me.”

A comma is not used in addition to a period, an exclamation mark, or a question mark.

15. To set off interjections.

You realize, of course, that I have no alternative.

You do want to go, don’t you?

I suppose you know, Mary, that I am engaged to Margaret.

Pu 5 SUPERFLUOUS COMMAS

Single commas should **not** be used in the following instances:

1. To separate a subject from its verb.

INCORRECT

The man in the red hat, is ludicrous.
(Omit the comma.)

2. To separate a verb from its object.

INCORRECT

This article says, that women are superior to men.
(Omit the comma.)

3. To separate a linking verb from a predicate noun or predicate adjective.

INCORRECT

Economics is obviously, not an exact science.
(Omit the comma.)

4. To separate a single adjective or the last adjective in a series from the word it modifies.

INCORRECT

John drives a blue, Chevrolet.
(Omit the comma.)

The coach looked approvingly at the tall, muscular, halfback.
(Omit the comma after *muscular.*)

Pu 6 COMMA SPLICE

A comma splice occurs when two independent clauses are separated only by a comma.

COMMA SPLICE

The sky darkened, it began to rain.

Ordinarily two independent clauses should be separated either by a mark of punctuation stronger than a comma or by a comma and a coordinate conjunction.

CORRECT

The sky darkened; it began to rain.

The sky darkened. It began to rain.

The sky darkened, and it began to rain.

A comma alone may sometimes be used between two independent clauses if the clauses are supposed to be read in quick succession or if their thought is closely related, but such punctuation is unorthodox and should be used rarely.

UNORTHODOX, BUT SOMETIMES ACCEPTABLE

Farming is not natural, it is an art.*

Special Problem

When a conjunctive adverb (*then, however, nevertheless*) is used at the beginning of the second independent clause, a semicolon or period is usually placed after the first clause.

It began to rain; nevertheless, we continued to play.

If the conjunctive adverb is *then,* there is an increasing tendency to use a comma.

The sky darkened, then it began to rain.

Those who prefer more conservative punctuation, however, would still use a semicolon or a period.

The sky darkened; then it began to rain.

The sky darkened. Then it began to rain.

Pu 7 DASH

A dash is used

1. To indicate a sudden break in the thought of a sentence.

I remember—but why bore you with my past?

2. To set off nonrestrictive information or comment (much in the manner of a parenthesis, but more strongly).

---

*Based on a sentence by Wendell Berry.

Palmer gauged the distance quickly—perhaps a little too quickly—and prepared to putt.

Note: Commas, parentheses, and dashes all set off nonrestrictive elements from the rest of the sentence, the comma indicating the weakest degree of separation and the dash the strongest. Commas or parentheses might have been used in the example above, but they would not have indicated as strong a degree of separation as the dashes.

3. To set off a series from a summarizing comment.

The choppy water, the rain, the disabled motor—all these added to our discomfort.

4. To set off final appositives.

For him there was only one sin—failure.

He stood admiring the produce—lettuce, potatoes, onions.

Note: A colon or, if there is only one appositive, a comma may also be used for this purpose.

Distinction between dashes and hyphens: In handwriting, a dash should be long enough to be distinguished from a hyphen. In typing, a dash is indicated by two hyphens with no space before or after them.

Caution: **Do not overuse dashes.** By providing means of suspending or breaking the main thought of the sentence, dashes may add greater flexibility to the structure of the sentence, but they should not be used as a careless substitute for other marks of punctuation. Dashes should not be used, for instance, to signal the end of a sentence or to provide an easy solution when you are in doubt about the kind of punctuation to use. Use dashes only for the purposes listed above, and even then do not use them frequently.

Note: No other mark of punctuation can properly precede or follow a dash.

INCORRECT

For him there was only one sin,—failure.

CORRECT

For him there was only one sin—failure.

Pu 8 ELLIPSIS

The ellipsis mark (three spaced periods) is used to indicate an omission from quoted material.

ORIGINAL STATEMENT

A good metaphor will produce a slight shock, a newness of perception. The meaning transcends the literal denotation of the words.

QUOTED WITH AN OMISSION

"A good metaphor will produce . . . a newness of perception. The meaning transcends the literal denotation of the words."

Note: A terminal mark of punctuation (such as a period) which comes just before or just after the omitted material is retained.

"A good metaphor will produce a slight shock. . . . The meaning transcends the literal denotation of the words." (Notice the four points—the ellipsis mark plus the period.)

Note: If the source of the quotation is clearly indicated, it is seldom necessary to use an ellipsis mark at the beginning or at the end of a quotation. Use common sense in deciding whether or not to retain internal punctuation (such as a comma) immediately before or after the omission.

Note: Extensive omissions (stanzas or many lines of poetry, several pages or paragraphs of prose) may be indicated by a line of periods, or by three or more periods centered on a line that is otherwise blank.

Pu 9 EXCLAMATION MARK

The exclamation mark is used after words or sentences expressing strong emotion or urgency.

Fire!

Look out for that car!

Pu 10 FUSED SENTENCE

Two independent clauses should be separated by a semicolon or a period, or by a comma and a coordinate conjunction. With no punctuation to separate them, the clauses run together, making the sentence difficult to read.

FUSED

He turned the ignition key the engine roared to life.

REVISED

He turned the ignition key; the engine roared to life.

He turned the ignition key. The engine roared to life.

He turned the ignition key, and the engine roared to life.

As he turned the ignition key, the engine roared to life. (Since the first clause has been subordinated by the insertion of a subordinate conjunction, a comma is sufficient.)

Pu 11 HYPHEN

Hyphens are used in compound words, in compound numbers from twenty-one to ninety-nine, and in words that are divided at the end of the line.

self-employed, forty-nine, prog-ress (when divided at the end of a line)

Compound words that are not hyphenated when used as nouns are usually hyphenated when used as adjectives.

We do not have air conditioning in our home.

We have installed an air-conditioning unit in our car.

In English, compounds characteristically change over a period of years: from two distinct words (base ball) to two words separated by a hyphen (base-ball) and finally to a single word (baseball). Before the compounds finally fuse, however, there may be a wide variety of usage at one particular time. When in doubt, consult a reputable dictionary.

Note: When it is necessary to divide a word at the end of a line, divide the word between syllables or between parts such as prefixes and suffixes. Consult your dictionary for the customary syllable division of the word. Use a hyphen after the part of the word at the end of the line.

Do not divide words of one syllable and do not separate a single letter from the rest of the word. If a word already contains a hyphen, divide the word at the point where the hyphen occurs.

INCORRECT

pro-ud, e-voke, read-y, self-evi-dent

CORRECT

proud, evoke, ready, self-evident

Pu 12 ITALICS

In handwriting or typing, the following are underlined with a single line to indicate that in print they are italicized:

1. Titles of books, periodicals, pamphlets, movies, plays, works of art, and long musical compositions.

Paradise Lost

The Reporter

Romeo and Juliet

Mr. Hulot's Holiday

New York Times

Tom Jones

Botticelli's Birth of Venus

Beethoven's Ninth Symphony

Note: Subordinate titles (chapter headings, short stories, individual essays, or poems which are printed as part of a larger work) require quotation marks, not underlining.

CORRECT

The first chapter of Life on the Mississippi is entitled "The River and Its History."

"Mending Wall" is the most famous poem in Robert Frost's book The Hired Man and Other People.

2. A word or letter used as a name for itself.

> *A* is the first letter of the alphabet.

3. Foreign words or phrases not yet assimilated into English. (When in doubt whether or not a word has been assimilated, consult your dictionary.)

> *coup de grace*
>
> *sui generis*

4. Names of ships, airplanes, trains, and spacecraft.

> *Spirit of Saint Louis*
>
> *Gemini 5*

5. Words that are intended to be emphatic. (Italics should rarely be used for this purpose.)

> Your sentences are *too* concise: a theme is not a telegram.

Pu 13 PARENTHESES

Parentheses are used to set off nonrestrictive information or comment.

> Palmer gauged the distance quickly (perhaps a little too quickly) and prepared to putt.

Note: Commas or dashes might have been used to set off the nonrestrictive comment. Commas would indicate a less emphatic separation; dashes, a more emphatic one.

Punctuation with Parentheses

1. If the material within the parenthesis is a complete sentence, the first word is capitalized and a period (or other appropriate terminal punctuation) is placed within the parenthesis. If such a parenthetical sentence occurs at the end of a sentence, the punctuation is as follows:

> The tank rumbled across the bridge. (Seconds later, the bridge was destroyed.)

If the parenthesis occurs at the end of the sentence and the material within the parenthesis is not a complete sentence, the terminal punctuation is placed outside the closing parenthesis (as in this sentence).

2. Within the sentence, commas or semicolons are sometimes used after the second parenthesis mark, but they are not used before the first parenthesis mark.

> A single shot rang out (a rifle shot); then the officer crumpled.

Pu 14 PERIOD

A period is used

1. To indicate the end of a sentence (declarative, imperative, or elliptical).

> The water was cold.
>
> Shut the door.
>
> Yes.

2. To indicate abbreviations.

B.C.

p.m.

Mr.

Dr.

Pu 15 QUESTION MARK

The question mark is used after every direct question.

Are you going?

Note: Indirect questions do not require a question mark.

He asked if I were going.

Pu 16 QUOTATION MARKS

Quotation marks are used

1. To enclose direct quotations.

The dying Kurtz exclaimed, ''The Horror! The Horror!''

2. To enclose a title published as a subordinate part under another title.

Webster's New World Dictionary contains a useful introductory section entitled ''Language and the Dictionary.''

3. To enclose words used ironically or words differing from their ordinary usage.

We had another ''calamity'' in the office today: we ran out of stamps.

Quotation marks should not be used frequently for this purpose. Many inexperienced writers use quotation marks as a kind of apology for trite words, slang phrases, or awkward colloquialisms.

> John is a ''great'' guy.

In such cases, dispense with the quotation marks and find a more exact word or phrase.

Pu 17 QUOTATIONS WITHIN QUOTATIONS

Quotations within quotations are enclosed in single quotation marks.

> John said quietly, ''I have always wondered why T. S. Eliot said 'April is the cruelest month.' ''

Pu 18 PUNCTUATION WITH QUOTATION MARKS

1. Commas and periods are placed within closing quotation marks.

> ''Horowitz is leading,'' he said, ''with three laps to go.'' (Notice that the comma after the word *leading* and the period at the end of the sentence are both placed within the quotation marks.)

2. Colons and semicolons are placed outside closing quotation marks.

> One student was reading ''Lycidas''; another was looking at the morning paper.

3. Question marks and exclamation marks are placed within closing quotation marks when they refer to the material within the quotation marks, outside when they refer to the sentence as a whole.

> Jane said, "Are you going?"
>
> Did the professor say, "Ben Jonson"?
>
> The crowd chanted, "Yankee go home!"
>
> One student was reading "Lycidas"!

4. When the preceding rule would require two final marks of punctuation (one referring to the material within the quotation marks and one referring to the sentence as a whole), only the first one is used.

> Did he say, "Are you going?"

Do not place a second question mark outside the closing quotation marks.

5. Interrupted quotations are punctuated as follows:

> "Spring is the time," he said, "when I become restless."

Note: If a mark of punctuation stronger than a comma would normally be required at the point of interruption, it is placed after the interrupting phrase.

> "April is exciting here," he said; "no place is more beautiful in the spring."

Note: A comma is *not* used in addition to a period, an exclamation mark, or a question mark.

> "Are you going?" she asked. "It should be an interesting party."

> ''I'm leaving!'' he shrieked. ''No one can stop me.''

6. Introductory statements which are not sentences are usually separated from a quotation by a comma. Introductory statements which are sentences are usually separated from a quotation by a colon.

> G. K. Chesterton once said, ''A good joke is the one ultimate and sacred thing which cannot be criticized.''
>
> G. K. Chesterton once made the following remark: ''A good joke is the one ultimate and sacred thing which cannot be criticized.''

Sometimes a short quotation is run into the sentence structure with no punctuation separating it from the rest of the sentence.

> G. K. Chesterton once said that a good joke is ''the one ultimate and sacred thing which cannot be criticized.''

Pu 19 CAPITALIZATION WITH QUOTATION MARKS

The first word of a quotation is capitalized unless the quotation is a single word or phrase that is blended into the sentence structure. See the examples in Pu 16–18.

Pu 20 LONG QUOTATIONS

Long quotations (more than three lines) are usually set off from the rest of the text by spatial arrangements such as indenting from both margins (or at least from the left margin) and, in typing, by single spacing. In such instances, no quotation marks are used.

> Suetonius cites the following examples of Caligula's madness:

> Next, Caligula extended the Palace as far as the Forum; converted the shrine of Castor and Pollux into a vestibule; and would often stand beside these Divine Brethren to be worshipped by all visitants, some of whom addressed him as 'Latian Juppiter.' He established a shrine to himself as God, with priests, the costliest possible victims and a life-sized golden image, which was dressed every day in clothes identical with those that he happened to be wearing. All the richest citizens tried to gain priesthoods here, either by influence or bribery. Flamingoes, peacocks, black grouse, guinea-hens, and pheasants were offered as sacrifices, each on a particular day of the month. When the moon shone full and bright he always invited the Moon-goddess to his bed; and during the day would indulge in whispered conversations with Capitoline Juppiter, pressing his ear to the god's mouth, and sometimes raising his voice in anger.*

Pu 21 SEMICOLON

A semicolon is used

1. Between independent clauses not joined by a coordinate conjunction.

> We left at noon; by three o'clock we were in Jackson.

Note: A series of very short independent clauses may be separated either by commas or by semicolons.

> We left early, we drove hard, we reached our destination on schedule.
>
> We left early; we drove hard; we reached our destination on schedule.

---

*Suetonius, *The Twelve Caesars,* trans. Robert Graves (Baltimore: Penguin Books, 1957), pp. 159–160.

2. Between two independent clauses joined by a coordinate conjunction (a) if the clauses are long, (b) if there are several commas within one of the clauses, or (c) if the writer wants a longer pause than would normally occur at the end of the first clause.

> Movies based on novels do not always follow the original as closely as the author or his admirers would like, even if the author is a consultant; but the movie may be thoroughly enjoyed by millions who have never read, and will never read, the novel.
>
> The clock struck as usual; but there was no one to hear.

3. Between two independent clauses when the second clause begins with a conjunctive adverb (*then, nevertheless, therefore*).

> We lay in the sun for an hour; then we swam out to the island.
>
> He seldom attended class; nevertheless, he was chagrined when he failed.

4. For clarity when punctuating items in a series.

> His summer itinerary included visits to New Orleans, Louisiana; Taos, New Mexico; and Rockland, Maine.

Pu 22 SEMICOLON FRAGMENT

A semicolon should not be used to separate a dependent clause or a phrase from the rest of the sentence.

> INCORRECT
>
> We left the stadium early; hoping to avoid the heavy traffic.

The quarterback lofted a long pass; just as the gun sounded. (In these examples the semicolon separates subordinate elements from the rest of the sentence too strongly.)

CORRECT

We left the stadium early, hoping to avoid the heavy traffic.

The quarterback lofted a long pass, just as the gun sounded.

The quarterback lofted a long pass just as the gun sounded.

Pu 23 CREATIVE PUNCTUATION

Sometimes an experienced writer will deliberately violate the conventions of standard punctuation to produce a special effect in a particular passage of prose. If he succeeds, he has shown that he has sufficient control of his language to go beyond the rules, as John Gardner does in the passage below.

> A country cemetery in upstate New York. Spring. The sky very blue, clouds very white. Trees, higher up the slope; this side of the trees an iron fence surrounding a cemetery; below the lower cemetery fence a broad valley, the Tonawanda Creek winding slowly and placidly like yellow mercury among willows. The pastureland on each side of the creek seems as smooth as a park from this distance. Two red barns, over by the highway, like barns in a painting.
>
> Nothing ever changes within the bounds of the iron fence: The grass grows green, explodes into field flowers, turns brown in September, bends under snow in the wintertime, grows green again; the sharp edges of chiseled names grow less sharp, mysteriously, year by year; birds build in the grass and trees, more each year, all the hawks and foxes dead; but nothing changes. Like sound waves on an empty planet, Nature's confusion spends itself unnoticed, or almost unnoticed. John Gardner, *The Resurrection*

Beginning writers should first be sure that they know the

rules before they try to violate them, but sometimes it is fun to experiment with unusual punctuation in a notebook or on a sheet of scratch paper.

Mechanics

M 1 ABBREVIATION

1. **Do not abbreviate** the names of states, countries, days, months, units of measure, or names of persons.

2. **In formal writing, do not abbreviate** the words *page, chapter, volume* (except in footnotes); words such as *street, avenue, company, corporation;* or titles such as *president* or *senator*.

3. **Names of organizations and government agencies are sometimes abbreviated** (especially when used frequently), usually without periods after each letter.

YMCA, TVA, GOP, FHA

M 2 CAPITALIZATION

Capitalize

1. **Proper nouns** (the names of unique persons, places, or things) **and adjectives** derived from proper nouns.

Sam Barnes, Rocky Mount, France, the Washington Monument, French, American, Miltonic

2. **Generic nouns** such as *river, mountain, street, school, park, captain, major* when they are used in conjunction with a proper noun or when they combine with another word to form a proper noun.

Grandfather Mountain, the Ohio River, Pine Street, Carrboro Elementary School, Umstead Park, Captain James Milligan

3. First words—of sentences, direct quotations, lines of poetry, and footnotes.

He will be there.
She asked, ''Are you sure?''
''Nature's first green is gold,
  Her hardest hue to hold.''
Ibid.

Exception: Fragmentary quotations are not capitalized.

Goldwater said that he was ''running scared.''

4. Words indicating family relationship—when they are not preceded by articles or possessive pronouns.

We visit Mother and Father every summer.

We visit my mother and father every summer.

5. All the words in titles except articles, prepositions, and conjunctions. Long prepositions and conjunctions (five or more letters) are sometimes also capitalized. The first and last words of titles are capitalized regardless of what part of speech they are.

The Heart of Darkness
By Love Possessed
''What Men Live By''
The Seed Beneath the Snow
A Long and Happy Life

6. Names of races or ethnic groups.

Indian, Eskimo, Caucasian

The capitalization of *Black* has not yet been standardized. It is usually capitalized when it is used as a noun referring to race, but it may or may not be capitalized when it is used as an adjective.

7. Names of historical events and periods.

the Gettysburg Address, the Battle of the Bulge, the Renaissance

8. *North, South, East,* and *West* when they refer to regions, but not when they refer to directions.

The South is rapidly becoming industrialized.

Our house faces south.

9. Names of specific courses.

Physics 104, Chemistry 211
but chemistry, physics, history

Note: Sometimes the following are capitalized: names of military organizations, areas of specialization, names of departments and committees within a large organization, philosophical or political systems, and new word coinages where no standard rule or usage has been established.

Army, Navy, Air Force, Sales Department, Fascism, the New Frontier, Medicare, the Cold War

M 3 FOOTNOTES AND ENDNOTES

The two main types of documentation are notes and bibliography. Notes, whether at the foot of the page (footnotes) or at the end of the paper or chapter (endnotes), are the elements of documentation that enable a reader to make a direct check of specific ideas, arguments, and quotations. Notes must therefore direct the reader to the exact passage the writer has used. An inaccurate page number can misdirect and exasperate the friendliest reader. A bibliography, on the other hand, is a general listing of works consulted. It differs in format from the notes, and it is always placed at the end of the paper. It may contain all the works consulted, or it may contain only those that the author believes are especially valuable; it must, however, include all of the works cited in the notes. Because notes and bibliographical entries have somewhat different purposes, they have different forms.

Notes, whether they are footnotes or endnotes, should be numbered consecutively throughout the paper or chapter. The number of the note should immediately follow the quotation or sentence to which it refers and should be set above the line.

> Jones argues that the work is "of no merit whatsoever."[1]

The number should also appear above the line in the note itself.

> [1]Jonah Jones, <u>Life at Sea</u> . . .

Footnotes should be single-spaced within the note, double-spaced between notes. Endnotes, on the other hand, are double-spaced both within and between notes.

The kind of note that comments on or expands the text should offer no problems. If you want to include information that is in the nature of an aside (but is too long for parenthetical inclusion in the text), you may insert it in a note in the normal sequence of notes. It is still cast in sentence form, but it will be spaced like the other notes. Sometimes a note of comment will also include documentary reference information. In such a case the information should follow as far as practicable the form for straight documentary notes:

[2]This same point is made by Albertus Magnus in his Summa Theologicae but without the intellectual sophistication demonstrated by Mrs. Roosevelt. See the excellent commentary on Albertus' deficiencies by James Baldwin, The Universal Fraud (New York: Madison Press, 1901), pp. 607-721.

Most notes will be of the documentary kind. These exist to direct the reader to a source that the writer used in forming his views or statements. Any direct quotation from another work must be documented in a note. Paraphrases and borrowed ideas should also be indicated in a note. However, it is not necessary to document ideas or facts that are common knowledge—for example, a statement that the United States lies in the Western Hemisphere. If an idea from an outside source permeates an entire paragraph, it is not necessary to have separate notes after each sentence. Instead, write one note for the whole paragraph, and put the note number at the end of the paragraph. Common sense will guide you in most cases, but if you think that your indebtedness to another work may not be clear to the reader, then use a note.

The documentary note is of two kinds—the first reference to a work and later references to the same source. The first reference to a work ought to give all information necessary for the reader to proceed directly to that work. Since slightly different forms apply for books, articles, and nonprinted media, they will be treated separately.

First References to Books

1. A book with one author, first edition.

   Edith Wharton, Ethan Frome (New York: Charles Scribner's Sons, 1911), p. 52.

2. A book with two authors, first edition.

James Agee and Walker Evans, Let Us Now Praise Famous Men (Boston: Houghton Mifflin, 1960), p. 151.

(This is a reprint of a book first published in 1939, but it is still the first edition.)

3. A later edition.

James Holly Hanford, A Milton Handbook, 4th ed. (New York: Appleton-Century-Crofts, 1961), p. 311.

4. A book with an author and an editor.

Mark Twain, Adventures of Huckleberry Finn, ed. Henry Nash Smith (Boston: Houghton Mifflin, 1958), p. 67.

5. A book of two or more volumes.

The Poems of John Donne, ed. H. J. C. Grierson (London: Oxford Univ. Press, 1912), II, 187-189.
(Notice that the volume number must be given. The abbreviations "vol." and "p." are superfluous in this case.)

6. An article from a book with an editor.

W. W. Robson, "The Better Fortitude," in The Living Milton, ed. Frank Kermode (London: Routledge & Kegan Paul, 1962), p. 132.

7. A book with a translator.

Gottfried Zeydel, The Youth of Conrad, trans. James Bright (Chapel Hill: Univ. of North Carolina Press, 1931), p. 79.

8. A book whose author is unknown.

Audiovisual Market Place: A Multimedia Guide (New York & London: R. R. Bowker, 1978), p. 17.

(Simply cite the information that you have, beginning with the title. Do not use *Anonymous* or *Anon.*)

9. A book with a corporate author.

    Commission to Revise the Tax Structure, Reforming the Federal Tax Structure (Washington, D.C.: Fund for Public Policy Research, 1973), p. 18.
    or
    Reforming the Federal Tax Structure, by the Commission to Revise the Tax Structure (Washington, D.C.: Fund for Public Policy Research, 1973), p. 18.

First References to Periodicals

1. An article in a scholarly journal.

    Helmut Hatzfield, "Use and Misuse of 'Baroque' As a Critical Term in Literary History," Univ. of Toronto Quarterly, 31 (1962), 180.

2. An article in a magazine.

    Walter Lippmann, "The Nuclear Age," Atlantic, May 1962, p. 46.
    (This is a monthly magazine.)

    David Bergamini, "The Language of Science," The Reporter, 31 March 1960, pp. 38-39.
    (This is a bi-monthly magazine.)

3. An unsigned article in an encyclopedia.

    "Birds of Paradise," Encyclopaedia Britannica (11th ed., 1910), II, 197.

4. An article in a newspaper.

"Community Colleges: An Important Innovation," The Chapel Hill Weekly, 14 June 1964, p. 4-B.

5. An unpublished dissertation.

Lawrence W. Hyman, "The Lyric Poetry of Andrew Marvell," unpublished Ph.D. dissertation (Columbia University, 1951), p. 38.

6. Pamphlets, bulletins, etc.

Geraldine Acker, Counting Your Calories, Univ. of Illinois Circular No. 790 (Urbana, Illinois, 1958), p. 8.

Camping by Car & Boat, Phillips Petroleum Company (Bartlesville, Oklahoma, 1962), p. 23.

Since the bibliographical information given by the publisher varies greatly from one pamphlet to another, no standard form can be given. List concisely the information that is given, using the models above insofar as possible.

First References to Nonprinted Media

Because of the varying nature of the information to be cited, notes for nonprinted media are not as uniform as those for books and periodicals. The following notes list only the most essential information. If further information is important to your discussion, simply add that material as concisely as possible after the title or at the end of the citation.

There is no need to provide documentary notes every time you mention a movie or a radio program in a short informal paper. In a research paper, however, you should try to document such references as fully as possible, using the models given here. The program credits pass by so quickly on the screen or on the radio that you may not be able to get everything written down. If that happens, you will simply have to use what you have.

Printed information about films can usually be obtained from reference works such as *Film Facts* or *The American Film Institute Catalogue of Motion Pictures,* but no such catalogues are available for radio and television programs. *TV Guide* and printed radio programs may be of some help, but so far no standard method of printed citation has been developed for radio and television.

Film

Feature-Length Films

Arthur Penn, dir., Bonnie and Clyde, Warner Brothers, 1967.

(It has become customary in filmography to list the name of the director before the title. If you are uncertain of the producer/distributor, that information may be omitted without seriously inconveniencing the reader. The title of a feature length film is underlined.)

Short films

Pare Lorentz, dir., "The River," U.S. Department of Agriculture, 1937.

(The title of a short film is placed within quotation marks. This film runs for thirty-two minutes.)

Television

"Man on Fire," Hawaii Five-O, CBS, 16 June 1978.

(The title of a particular program is placed within quotation marks; the title of a regular series is underlined. It is not always necessary to list the station on which you viewed a network program. The station should be listed, however, when such information is needed to identify a non-network program.)

"Willa Cather's America," PBS special, WUNC-TV, Chapel Hill, N.C., 9 May 1978.
(Since the time and date of PBS programs are decided by individual stations rather than by the PBS network, it is necessary to list a specific station if the date is given.)

The General Assembly Today, Univ. of North Carolina Television Network, 16 June 1978.
(This program, which is a regular feature on Tuesday through Friday when the state legislature is in session, was shown only by the University of North Carolina Television Network.)

Radio

"Community Control of Schools," Options in Education, National Public Radio, WUNC radio, Chapel Hill, N.C., 26 June 1978.
(Since the time of presentation of NPR programs varies from station to station, a specific station is listed.)

"Meet the Candidates," WCHL radio, Chapel Hill, N.C., 25 April 1978.
(This was a one-time program presenting local candidates for political office.)

Cassette tapes

Henry A. Kissinger, Foreign Policy—The Kissinger View, a cassette tape, Santa Barbara, Calif., Center for the Study of Democratic Institutions, 1974.

Margaret Ranald, Women in Shakespeare's

Tragedies, a lecture on cassette tape, Everett/Edwards, n.d.
(The dates of cassette tapes are often unavailable; *n.d.* means *no date.*)

If the subject is not made clear by the title or by the context, it may be necessary to add a brief description:

Gilbert Highet, The Stationary Man, a discussion of Gilbert White's The Natural History of Selbourne, a cassette tape, Jeffrey Norton, n.d.

Phonograph records

Bob Dylan, "Maggie's Farm," from Hard Rain, Columbia Records, 1976.

Huey P. Newton, Huey Newton Speaks, Paredon Records, 1971. Interviewed July 4, 1970, by Mark Lane in the California State Prison at San Luis Obispo.

Lectures

Muriel C. Bradbrook, "The Commonwealth of Poets: Shakespeare and His Fellow Elizabethans," a lecture given at the Folger Shakespeare Library, Washington, D.C., 24 April 1978.

Robert Bain, Professor of English, classroom lecture, Univ. of North Carolina, fall semester, 1979.

Interviews

Norman Mailer, personal interview, 13 June 1978.

If the person being interviewed is not generally known, it may be helpful to identify his title or profession.

William Harmon, Undersecretary, Department of the Interior, Washington, D.C., personal interview, 17 April 1978.

Robert Haig, economist, Brookings Institute, telephone interview, 3 October 1977.

If you have taped an interview or lecture, that fact should be mentioned because it would add greater authenticity to the material. You could use the words "classroom lecture on tape" or "personal interview on tape." Or you might simply place the word *taped* within parentheses at what seems to be the most appropriate place in the citation. You would not, of course, tape an interview without permission, nor would you publish it in transcribed form or play it for a large audience without permission.

Unpublished letters

Hunter Thompson, personal letter, 4 Oct. 1976.

Robert Donaldson, letter to Thomas Ruffin, 24 Jan. 1846, Thomas Ruffin Papers, in the Southern Historical Collection, Univ. of North Carolina Library, Chapel Hill.

Second References to Books and Periodicals

Since second references allude to works already cited in full in first references, they are considerably briefer than first references. The most common second reference is *ibid.* (capitalized if it begins the entry, and followed by a period).

Ibid., p. 47.

Ibid. means "in the same place," and it is used only to refer to a work cited in the *immediately preceding note*. If another work has intervened, *ibid.* may not be used. In such a case use the author's last name and the page number to which this note refers:

Jones, p. 47.

If more than one work by the same author has been cited, use a short form of the title of the particular work by the author you are referring to:

Jones, Second Coming, p. 89.

There is no need to repeat in the note material that has been given in the main body of the text—for example, if you cite the name of the author or the full title of the book in the text, there is no need to repeat that information in the note; only the remaining information required for a standard note should be given in the note.

Second References to Nonprinted Media

Since page numbers cannot be cited for unpublished materials, references to them cannot be as precise as those for printed materials. When second references are made to nonprinted materials, your main concern should be to make it as easy as possible for the reader to find the first reference or the bibliographical entry. Precise forms cannot be given for every possibility, but try to be as brief as is consistent with clarity. In the second reference to a film, for instance, simply cite the title, or in the second reference to a lecture, cite the name of the lecturer and as much of the title as is necessary to identify it.

[5]Bonnie and Clyde.

[18]Bradbrook, "The Commonwealth of Poets."

M 4 BIBLIOGRAPHY

Research papers almost invariably carry a bibliography at the end. The bibliography may list all of the works consulted, in which case it is often entitled *A List of Works Consulted*, or it may list only items that the author has used or that he thinks would be useful to the reader, in which case it is entitled *A Selected Bibliography*. It should always list all of the works cited in the footnotes.

The works are listed alphabetically by the last name of the author or, if the author is unknown, by the first word in the title (disregarding *a*, *an*, or *the*). The indentation, which differs from that of footnotes, is indicated in the sample entries that follow. Note carefully the difference in format between the bibliographical entries and the notes in M 3.

Acker, Geraldine. Counting Your Calories. Univ. of Illinois Circular No. 790. Urbana, Illinois, 1958.

Agee, James, and Walker Evans. Let Us Now Praise Famous Men. Boston: Houghton Mifflin, 1960.

Audiovisual Market Place: A Multimedia Guide. New York & London: R. R. Bowker, 1978.

Bain, Robert, Professor of English. Classroom lecture, Univ. of North Carolina, fall semester, 1979.

Bergamini, David. "The Language of Science." The Reporter, 31 March 1960, pp. 36-40.

"Birds of Paradise." Encyclopaedia Britannica (11th ed., 1910), II, 197-198.

Bradbrook, Muriel C. "The Commonwealth of Poets: Shakespeare and His Fellow Elizabethans." A lecture given at the Folger Shakespeare Library, Washington, D.C., 24 April 1978.

Camping by Car & Boat. Bartlesville, Oklahoma: Phillips Petroleum Company, 1962.

Commission to Revise the Tax Structure. Reforming the Federal Tax Structure. Washington, D.C.: Fund for Public Policy Research, 1973.

"Community Colleges: An Important Innovation." The Chapel Hill Weekly, 14 June 1964, p. 4-B.

"Community Control of Schools." Options in Education. National Public Radio. WUNC radio, Chapel Hill, N.C. 26 June 1978.

Donaldson, Robert. Letter to Thomas Ruffin, 24 Jan. 1846. Thomas Ruffin Papers, in the Southern Historical Collection, Univ. of North Carolina Library, Chapel Hill.

Dylan, Bob. "Maggie's Farm." From Hard Rain. Columbia Records, 1976.

The General Assembly Today. Univ. of North Carolina Television Network. 16 June 1978.

Haig, Robert, economist, Brookings Institute. Telephone interview. 3 October 1977.

Hanford, James Holly. A Milton Handbook, 4th ed. New York: Appleton-Century-Crofts, 1961.

Harmon, William, Undersecretary, Department of the Interior, Washington, D.C. Personal interview. 17 April 1978.

Hatzfield, Helmut. "Use and Misuse of 'Baroque' As a Critical Term in Literary History." Univ. of Toronto Quarterly, 31 (1962), 180-200.

Highet, Gilbert. The Stationary Man. A discussion of Gilbert White's The Natural History of Selbourne. A cassette tape. Jeffrey Norton, n.d.

Hyman, Lawrence W. "The Lyric Poetry of Andrew Marvell." Unpublished Ph.D. dissertation (Columbia University, 1951).

Kissinger, Henry A. Foreign Policy—The Kissinger View. A cassette tape. Santa Barbara, Calif.: Center for the Study of Democratic Institutions, 1974.

Lippmann, Walter. "The Nuclear Age." Atlantic, May 1962, pp. 46-48.

Lorentz, Pare, dir. "The River." U.S. Department of Agriculture, 1937.

Mailer, Norman. Personal interview. 13 June 1978.

"Man on Fire." Hawaii Five-O. CBS. 16 June 1978.

"Meet the Candidates." WCHL radio, Chapel Hill, N.C. 25 April 1978.

Newton, Huey P. Huey Newton Speaks. Paredon Records, 1971.

Penn, Arthur, dir. Bonnie and Clyde. Warner Brothers, 1967.

The Poems of John Donne. Ed. H. J. C. Grierson. 2 vols. London: Oxford Univ. Press, 1912.

Ranald, Margaret. Women in Shakespeare's Tragedies. A lecture on cassette tape. Everett/Edwards, n.d.

Robson, W. W. "The Better Fortitude." In The Living Milton. Ed. Frank Kermode. London: Routledge & Kegan Paul, 1962, pp. 124-137.

Thompson, Hunter. Personal letter. 4 Oct. 1976.

Twain, Mark. Adventures of Huckleberry Finn. Ed. Henry Nash Smith. Boston: Houghton Mifflin, 1958.

Wharton, Edith. Ethan Frome. New York: Charles Scribner's Sons, 1911.

"Willa Cather's America." PBS Special. WUNC-TV, Chapel Hill, N.C. 9 May 1978.

Zeydel, Gottfried. The Youth of Conrad. Trans. James Bright. Chapel Hill: Univ. of North Carolina Press, 1931.

M 5 NUMBERS

Technical or scientific journals and newspapers tend to use arabic numerals (5, 10, 21, etc.) to represent numbers, whereas the more general procedure is to use words (five, ten, twenty-one) for numbers that can be written in one or two words and arabic numerals for numbers that require more than two words.

Unless you are writing for a publication with a specified procedure, you should follow the general practice of using words for numbers from one to one hundred and arabic numerals for larger numbers. In a passage with extensive numbers, however, all publications tend to use arabic numerals to save space.

> Royal Gorge Bridge, 1,053 feet above the Arkansas River in Colorado, is the highest bridge above water. Opened on December 8, 1925, it is 1,260 feet long, with a main span of 880 feet and a width of 18 feet.

The guidelines that follow are offered for help in exceptional cases.

1. A number placed at the beginning of a sentence is usually written in words.

> Forty-one students have registered for the course.

2. Arabic numerals are used for dates, street and room numbers, time with a.m. or p.m., decimals, percentages, and pages of books.

January 4, 1962	.005
April 17 (do not use *th*)	8 percent (or 8%)
Room 207	page 116
113 Park Place	4:04 a.m.

3. When two numbers appear in succession, one of them is written in words.

ten 4-ply tires

twenty-five ¼-inch bolts

4. When they are written as words, compound numbers from 21 to 99 are spelled with a hyphen.

twenty-one

ninety-nine

5. Fractions are usually spelled out, with a hyphen between the numerator and the denominator.

The semester is *three-fourths* gone.

However, there are some exceptions. Fractions used to give measurements or dimensions tend to be written in arabic numerals, especially when there are several fractions in a passage.

The underpass had a clearance of 13½ feet.

Finished two by fours actually measure 1½ inches by 3½ inches.

I bought a ¾-inch drill.

When *one-half* is used as a noun, it is sometimes written without a hyphen.

One half of the cake is missing.

(*But:* He is *one-half* Indian.)

If a passage contains a large number of fractions, arabic numerals may be used to save space.

6. Ordinal numbers (*first, second,* etc.) are usually designated by words rather than by numerals.

The earth is the *fifth* largest planet and the *third* from the sun.

7. Sums of money are indicated by arabic numerals ($12.37) unless they are small enough to be written in two or three words (twelve dollars, thirty-six francs), in which case either numerals or words may be used.

Spelling

Sp 1 SPELLING RULES

1. Use *i* before *e* except after *c* or when pronounced as *a* (as in *eight*).

CORRECT

believe, receive, vein

EXCEPTIONS

leisure, seize, weird, foreign

2. A final *e* is usually omitted before a suffix beginning with a vowel and retained before a suffix beginning with a consonant.

CORRECT

hope + *ing* becomes *hoping*

hope + *ful* becomes *hopeful*

EXCEPTIONS

argument, awful, duly, truly

changeable, noticeable (to retain the soft *c* and *g*)

3. When adding a suffix beginning with a vowel (*-ing*, *-ed*) to a word ending in a single consonant preceded by an *accented* vowel (*begín*, *occúr*), double the final consonant (*beginning*, *occurred*).

Note: The final consonant is *not* doubled (a) if it is preceded by a double vowel: *looking*, *reaping*, *seeming;* (b) if the vowel preceding it is not accented: *bénefited*, *háppening*, *óffering*.

4. When adding a suffix to a word ending in *y*, change the *y* to *i*.

> *happy* + *ness* becomes *happiness*
>
> *study* + *ed* becomes *studied*

But if the *y* is preceded by a vowel (as in *play*) or if the suffix begins with an *i* (as in *-ing*), the *y* is retained without change.

> *play* + *ful* becomes *playful*
>
> *study* + *ing* becomes *studying*
>
> EXCEPTIONS
>
> lay, laid; pay, paid; say, said

5. When a prefix ends with the same letter that the root word begins with, retain both letters.

> roommate, unnecessary, misspell

6. To form the plural add *s* to the singular unless the plural is pronounced with an additional syllable. If the plural acquires an extra syllable, add *es*.

> bag, bags
>
> church, churches

For more detailed information on the spelling of plurals (e.g., on exceptions such as *mice, deer, minutiae, alumni, data*), consult the special section on plurals in your dictionary.

IMPROVING YOUR SKILLS

Correcting Misspelled Words

When a misspelled word is pointed out to you,

1. Consult your dictionary to determine the correct spelling.

2. Using a phonetic guide in your dictionary, pronounce the word slowly several times—first, syllable by syllable; then as a whole.
3. Print the word, capitalizing the part that is most likely to cause trouble: sepArate, sacriLEGious, suRprise.
4. Use any device that will help you to remember the correct spelling: There is A RAT in SEPARATE, LOOSE rhymes with GOOSE, etc.
5. Write the word in larger than normal letters. Then trace over the word several times as you say the word to yourself.
6. Keep a list of words that you have misspelled. If a word occurs on this list more than once, make a special effort to memorize its correct form.

A List of Frequently Misspelled Words

The following words are frequently misspelled. Try to spell them correctly as someone reads them to you. Memorize the words that you miss; then take the test again. Continue this procedure until you can spell all of the words correctly.

absence	among	breathe	conquer
accidentally	anxiety	business	conscience
accommodate	apparent	candidate	conscious
achievement	appearance	ceiling	dealt
acknowledge	argument	certain	definite
acquaint	article	changeable	describe
acquire	athlete	clothes	despair
across	audience	coarse	desperate
address	auxiliary	column	disastrous
aisle	beginning	coming	divine
already	believe	concede	eighth
altogether	benefited	conceive	embarrass

environment
equipped
exaggerate
exceed
excellent
exhaust
existence
experience
extreme
familiar
fascinate
February
fiery
fifth
foreign
fourth
forty
friend
goddess
government
grammar
grievous
guard
guidance
height
hindrance
huge
humorous
hurriedly
imaginary
immediately
instance
instants

intercede
interest
its
it's (it is)
irrelevant
knowledge
laboratory
later
latter
lead
led
loose
lose
losing
maintenance
maneuver
marriage
meant
medicine
miniature
minute
mischievous
misspelled
moral
morale
mysterious
necessary
neither
niece
ninety
ninth
noticeable

obstacle
occasion
occurred
opinion
opportunity
optimistic
paid
parallel
pastime
perceive
perform
perhaps
permissible
personal
personnel
possession
precede
preference
principal
principle
privilege
probably
proceed
pronunciation
prove
psychology
pursuit
quantity
quiet
quite
receive
recommend

regard
referring
rhythm
sacrilegious
seize
sense
separate
shining
similar
studying
stretch
strictly
success
surprise
thorough
till
tragedy
trouble
truly
undoubtedly
until
usually
vacuum
valuable
vegetable
villain
weak
Wednesday
weird
whether
writing
written

Paragraphs

A paragraph is a group of sentences constituting a unit of thought or emphasis. It is characterized typographically by the indentation of the first line from the left margin.

One virtue of the paragraph is that it allows you to concentrate on one aspect of the subject at a time. Particularly in short forms such as themes, letters, or reports, you might profitably develop the habit of thinking of the overall organization in terms of the number and arrangement of the paragraphs. After blocking out the whole theme in terms of paragraphs, you are free to concentrate on one paragraph at a time, developing each as fully and cogently as possible.

The remarks that follow apply primarily to expository paragraphs. Narrative and descriptive paragraphs may make use of these principles and methods, but frequently they simply indicate a change in perspective or a turn in the action, or emphasize certain details by isolating them in a separate paragraph. The only strongly established convention in narrative and descriptive paragraphs concerns the use of dialogue: when dialogue is used, a new paragraph is begun each time there is a change of speakers.

In expository or argumentative writing, where the main concern is presenting a clear progression of thought, conventional usage is more definitely established, and several guidelines may be followed with confidence. The following principles in particular are helpful in writing good expository and argumentative paragraphs.

Pa 1 CHARACTERISTICS OF GOOD PARAGRAPHS

1. Unity. A paragraph should contain one central idea which unifies all of the individual sentences. A simple but very effective device for ensuring unity is the topic sentence, which states the central idea of the paragraph. The topic sentence clarifies the purpose of the paragraph and serves as a guide to what should be included. If you are having trouble with paragraph development, you should form the habit of writing a topic sentence for every paragraph and placing it near the beginning of the paragraph. Once this habit has been developed, you will find that you can conceive of the central idea of the paragraph without actually writing it down. You can also begin to experiment with placement of the topic sentence at various points in the paragraph.

The paragraph below is a perfect little unit and has no need of further development, but the author could easily expand it by simply adding further examples. The first sentence focuses the thought; the following sentences develop it.

> Sounds do not always give us pleasure according to their sweetness and melody; nor do harsh sounds always displease. We are more apt to be captivated or disgusted with the associations which they promote, than with the sounds themselves. Thus the shrilling of the field-cricket, though sharp and stridulous, yet marvellously delights some hearers, filling their minds with a train of summer ideas of everything that is rural, verduous, and joyous. Gilbert White, *The Natural History of Selborne*

2. Coherence. Coherence means that the thought contained in one sentence should be clearly related to the thought of the following sentence. There should be no awkward or excessively abrupt transitions. The following devices are useful in achieving coherence between sentences:

1. A pronoun in one sentence referring to a word in the preceding sentence.
2. Repetition of key words, if used sparingly.
3. Transitional words or phrases, such as *furthermore, yet, nevertheless, in addition, for example, but.*

More important than these mechanical devices, however, is a clear logical progression of thought from one sentence to the next. If the logical relationship is present, there will not usually be problems of coherence. Occasionally, however, a transitional word or phrase, such as those in number 3 above, may be useful in lessening an impression of abruptness.

Study the ways in which coherence is achieved between the sentences in the paragraph below. In addition to the coherence of thought, can you point out specific linking devices that are used to ensure smooth transitions from one sentence to the next?

> Always, in the past, war and the threat of war, whether aggressive or defensive, were usable instruments. They were usable instruments in the sense that nations could go to war for their national purposes. Nations could transform themselves from petty states to great powers by means of war. They could enlarge their territories, acquire profitable colonies, change the religion of a vanquished population, all by means of war. War was the instrument with which the social, political, and legal systems of large areas were changed. Thus, in the old days before the nuclear age began, war was a usable—however horrible and expensive—instrument of national purpose. The reason for that was that the old wars could be won. Walter Lippmann, "The Nuclear Age"

3. Adequate development. One common failing of inexperienced writers is a persistent tendency to write short, underdeveloped paragraphs. Sometimes a short, emphatic paragraph is remarkably effective. But if all or most of your paragraphs are two to four sentences in length, then you are probably doing one of two things: you are being too broad and general, or you are failing to develop your ideas as fully as you should. The solution is not to pad your paragraph by inserting a few more words in each sentence or by adding repetitious statements, but to delve into the idea more thoroughly through the inclusion of more details. Be more specific. Examine the subject more thoroughly; explain it more fully.

For good examples of paragraphs that are adequately developed, look at several of the paragraphs in Pa 2.

4. Variety. Paragraphs, like sentences, should not be monotonously uniform; occasional variety is invigorating. Short paragraphs are more emphatic than longer ones, but they depend for their full effect upon a contrast with longer paragraphs. A series of short, emphatic paragraphs would be just as monotonous as an unrelieved succession of long ones.

Pa 2 METHODS OF PARAGRAPH DEVELOPMENT

A paragraph is more than just a random typographical indentation to indicate a strong pause. It is an intermediate unit of thought—longer than a sentence, shorter than a theme—with an integrity of its own. The indentations merely indicate the spatial limits. Internally, a paragraph can be, to appropriate a phrase from John Donne, "a little world made cunningly." Most of the comments that follow relate to the "inside" of paragraphs, but a paragraph's relationship to the "outside"—that is, to the paragraphs coming before and after it—should not be forgotten. Each paragraph should fit smoothly into the whole paper, as one step on a particular stairway.

There is no simple formula for writing a good paragraph. Every good paragraph is unique. There are, however, some things that you can do to become more aware of the possible ways of using paragraphs. And if you are willing to work at it, there is no reason why you can't learn to write effective paragraphs consistently. A good beginning would be to learn to recognize and use the basic patterns listed below.

1. Space order: the ordering of a paragraph primarily in terms of movement through space. *Perspective* (the point from which something is seen, as a photograph is seen from the perspective of the camera lens) and *selection* (what the camera focuses on, as opposed to what it excludes or glides over) are important here. The perspective can be fixed or moving. A *fixed perspective*, for instance, might describe the campus as seen from a classroom window. Since you could not describe every minute facet of what you saw, you would have to select certain details, and you would be wise to present them in some easily followed order, such as from far to near, or in order of their prominence. A *moving perspective* could leave the classroom and describe what you would see as you left the building and walked about the campus. In this case it would be necessary to clearly inform the reader of the route taken by mentioning occasional landmarks and by indicating the direction from which they were approached. If the direction of the movement is not clear, the reader may become confused.

Sometimes the space orientation is limited to a few simple directional phrases, sometimes it is rather detailed, but it should always remain in the background. The movement itself should never be so complex as to distract the reader from what is being described or talked about.

Space ordering can have many variant forms. Here are two relatively simple ones:

> They walked down a hall away from the dining room past silent nurses. At the end of the hall was a door that led to the outside. They went out and she told him that often she went out to sit on the brick wall on the small patio and to feel the sun on her face. She smiled with pride as she showed him her tiny bit of happiness. There was a driveway near the patio, and the earth sloped to a shallow spot where trash and sludge collected. It was filthy, yet she could feel the sun there. Chip Moore, Student Theme (The next paragraph begins, "On the way back to the dining room. . . .")

> The caravan seemed a miserably frail and Lilliputian thing as it crept over the boundless prairie toward the sky line. Of road or trail

> there lay not a trace ahead; as soon as the grass had straightened up again behind, no one could have told the direction from which it had come or whither it was bound. The whole train—Per Hansa with his wife and children, the oxen, the waggons, the cow, and all—might just as well have dropped down out of the sky. Nor was it at all impossible to imagine that they were trying to get back there again; their course was always the same—straight toward the west, straight toward the sky line. O. E. Rölvagg, *Giants in the Earth* (translated by Rölvagg and Lincoln Colcord)

2. Time order. In speaking of a time sequence, we usually mean presenting events in the order in which they occurred. But there are many ways of relating events in time. You are not forced to present your material in a continuous, unbroken flow. October of this year may be compared with October of last year, and even (hypothetically) with October of next year. Or instead of moving from the past to the present, you may decide to move from the present to the past. Within a given segment of time, however, the events must be presented in the order of their occurrence if they are to be intelligible.

Most paragraphs have some kind of chronological arrangement, but in some paragraphs the time order is so prominent that it provides the most obvious pattern of organization.

> One day the first prematurely senile leaf will quietly detach itself in a faint breeze and flutter silently to the ground. All through the summer an occasional unnoticed, unregretted leaf has fallen from time to time. But not as this one falls. There is something quietly ominous about the way in which it gives up the ghost, without a struggle, almost with an air of relief. Others will follow, faster and faster. Soon the ground will be covered, though many of the stubborner trees are still clothed. Then one night a wind, a little harder than usual, and carrying perhaps the drops of a cold rain, will come. We shall awake in the morning to see that the show is over. The trees are naked; bare, ruined choirs, stark against the sky. Joseph Wood Krutch, *The Twelve Seasons*

Caution: Notice, however, that the chronological pattern alone does not account for the paragraph's success. The vivid imagery and phrasing and the sense of a completed pattern contribute strongly to the total effect. Time order may provide the necessary framework of a paragraph, but time order alone is not enough. The events must be presented in an interesting manner, and they must form some kind of meaningful whole. A mere chronological list (I got out of bed and went to the bathroom. Then I went to breakfast, and then . . . etc.) is the easiest kind of writing because you don't have to think very hard about it, but it is usually very boring. In the welter of experience, you must be selective. Eliminate unimportant details and concentrate on the most important actions in the sequence.

3. Cumulative details: the cumulative presentation of facts, examples, reasons, or specific details in support of the central idea of the paragraph. The central idea of the paragraph is usually stated in a topic sentence, but not always. When a topic sentence is used, it may be placed at various points in the paragraph, although it is most frequently found at the beginning.

In the first paragraph below, the topic sentence is placed at the end, so that the paragraph moves from the presentation of a number of specific details to a concluding generalization.

In the second paragraph below, the beginning topic idea is reemphasized at the end. Although many of the images throughout the paragraph are quite detailed, Thoreau uses several clauses in the paragraph to echo the topic idea so that we never lose sight of it by being distracted by his sharp images.

The third paragraph below has no topic sentence; its unity is that of a picture in which all of the details combine to form a clear impression of one time, place, and action. It also receives a certain unity from the fact that it is one stage in a well-organized process.

Pressure pounded on my eardrums and an icy current of water swirled suddenly about my legs as I sank ankle-deep into the soft mud of the lake bottom. The homemade diving helmet, resting securely upon my shoulders, was now very light in comparison to its weight on the surface. The monotonous and steady "whuff, whuff" of the compressed air entering the helmet reminded me of the small two-cylinder hand pump and of my friends twenty feet above me on the surface. Darkness enveloped me; I thought of the dazzling brilliance of the June sun shining on the smooth water above—of the world that I had departed from only a few minutes before. It was my first experience in diving, and I didn't know whether to enjoy it or not. Roger Bullard, Student Theme

Our village life would stagnate if it were not for the unexplored forests and meadows which surround it. We need the tonic of wildness,—to wade sometimes in marshes where the bittern and the meadow-hen lurk, and hear the booming of the snipe; to smell the whispering sedge where only some wilder and more solitary fowl builds her nest, and the mink crawls with its belly close to the ground. At the same time that we are earnest to explore and learn all things, we require that all things be mysterious and unexplorable, that land and sea be infinitely wild, unsurveyed and unfathomed by us because unfathomable. We can never have enough of nature. We must be refreshed by the sight of inexhaustible vigor, vast and titanic features, the sea-coast with its wrecks, the wilderness with its living and its decaying trees, the thunder-cloud, and the rain which lasts three weeks and produces freshets. We need to witness our own limits transgressed, and some life pasturing freely where we never wander. Henry David Thoreau, *Walden*

Tethered to the slimy pier, ten commercial fishing boats bob up and down in the foamy, green salt water. Sea gulls screech and swoop down over the boats in eager anticipation. A steady stream of salmon is being unloaded from the holds and carried into the cannery. The fishermen never look up from their work, but continually jab at the seething mass of glittering salmon and toss them one after another onto the cluttered pier which is strewn with hoses, slabs of dirty ice, and puddles of blood. Men in rubber hip boots select the salmon to be immediately canned and flip them onto moving ladders. They then pile the low grade salmon and halibut, which have wandered into the nets by mistake, into blood-stained carts to be rolled off to the freezers. Glenna Middleton, Student Theme

4. Illustration. The use of a detailed example or examples to convince the reader of the truth of a generalization. For instance, in support of the generalization "Plains, Georgia, has been transformed by the election of Jimmy Carter as president," you might describe a scene on the main street of Plains, showing how a quiet village has been changed into a tourist mecca. Usually this method would involve one extended example, but you could develop a paragraph by giving many examples which would cumulatively support your generalization.

Here is a good example of a paragraph developed by illustration: a generalization followed by an extended illustration.

> In the Middle East, Americans usually have a difficult time with Arabs. I remember an American agriculturalist who went to Egypt to teach modern agricultural methods to the Egyptian farmers. At one point in his work he asked his interpreter to ask a farmer how much he expected his field to yield that year. The farmer responded by becoming very excited and angry. In an obvious attempt to soften the reply the interpreter said, "He says he doesn't know." The American realized something had gone wrong, but he had no way of knowing what. Later I learned that the Arabs regard anyone who tries to look into the future as slightly insane. When the American asked him about his future yield, the Egyptian was highly insulted since he thought the American considered him crazy. To the Arab only God knows the future, and it is presumptuous even to talk about it. Edward T. Hall, *The Silent Language*

5. Comparison and contrast: a comparison between two or more subjects in order to explain or clarify the nature of each. The subjects of the comparison may be discussed alternately within the same paragraph (as in the first paragraph below); or they may be discussed in separate paragraphs—first one being developed fully, then the other (see the second selection below). This second method is usually easier to handle than the first.

> Plato's ideal is reason; Dostoevsky's is love. Each idea is a true reflection of the ideals of the society of its author. The Greeks worshiped reason. They believed that through reason man could achieve an ideal existence, just as Plato's man is able to find the final good through reason. Christians, on the other hand, believe that man can attain his ideal existence, eternal life, through love and service to God, just as Raskolnikov began to build a better life with his new-found faith and humility. Neither the Greek or Christian ideal, however, has been embodied in a whole society. Only a relatively small number of individuals have been able to reach either of these two high goals. Kathleen Galway, Student Theme

> It is difficult tor most ot the persons who live in modern industrial societies to comprehend the struggle for mere existence that even today confronts many of the peoples of the world. In a modern urban society located in a favorable region the majority of people may live out their lives without ever having been threatened with uncontrolled natural forces. In fact, the average urban dweller of the Western world is so many times removed from direct contact with his natural environment that he is scarcely aware of its existence, much less of its importance to him. Our foods are packaged, canned, frozen, and often pre-cooked or ready to serve, and our clothing is likely to come to us ready made. Even the responsibility of heating our houses is increasingly a matter of adjusting a thermostat. In spite of the popular interest in do-it-yourself projects, if we are modern urban dwellers we are insulated from our environment by an array of gadgets and an army of professionals who serve as middlemen between us and the source of supplies on which all human lives depend.

> It is otherwise with the many peoples of the world who must deal more directly with the land or the sea. To many peoples eating meat means killing and dressing domestic animals, wild game, or fish which they have raised, hunted, or caught. Vegetable foods come to

them as a result of their labors in gardens, field, or forest; and such products must often be shucked, pounded, ground, or otherwise laboriously treated before they can be cooked and eaten. Most of the peoples of the world can now buy cloth, but the garments may still have to be cut and sewed at home. Houses in many parts of the world still require the cutting of trees or the making of bricks or thatch by local labor. In many of the simpler cultures firewood is still brought daily from the forest and water from a stream or the village well. Moreover, in many areas of the world people must wrestle with extremes of heat or cold, with droughts or floods and sometimes with both in the course of a single year. They may have to cope with poor soil or dense jungle growth. They may live in areas where domestic animals cannot be kept or where parasites, insects, and predatory animals threaten health and life.
Ina Corinne Brown, *Understanding Other Cultures*

6. Cause and effect: a progression from cause to effect, or from effect to cause. You may begin with an action and then show its consequences, or you may begin with the consequences and then examine their most significant causes. For instance, in developing the idea of "Industrial Pollution of Our Streams," you might begin with a description of a polluted stream and then examine the causes, or you might begin with an account of the disposal of industrial waste and then examine the consequences.

7. Definition: a statement of what a thing is. Usually a definition places its subject in a general class (*genus*) of things (a helmet is a *covering*), then distinguishes it from other members of that class (a helmet is a *protective* covering *for the head*). An extended definition might go on to distinguish between different kinds of helmets and to discuss each in detail. In other words, a definition can be a sentence, a paragraph, or a rather long essay, depending upon how extensively it is developed.

Sometimes a thing is defined by what it is not, as in the example below.

I ought first of all to explain that when I use the term history I mean knowledge of history. No doubt throughout all past time there actually occurred a series of events which, whether we know what it was or not, constitutes history in some ultimate sense. Nevertheless, much the greater part of these events we can know nothing about, not even that they occurred; many of them we can know only imperfectly; and even the few events that we think we know for sure we can never be absolutely certain of, since we can never revive them, never observe or test them directly. The event itself once occurred, but as an actual event it has disappeared; so that in dealing with it the only objective reality we can observe or test is some material trace which the event has left—usually a written document. With these traces of vanished events, these documents, we must be content since they are all we have; from them we infer what the event was, we affirm that it is a fact that the event was so and so. We do not say "Lincoln is assassinated"; we say "it is a fact that Lincoln was assassinated." The event *was,* but is no longer; it is only the affirmed fact about the event that *is,* that persists, and will persist until we discover that our affirmation is wrong or inadequate. Let us then admit that there are two histories: the actual series of events that once occurred; and the ideal series that we affirm and hold in memory. The first is absolute and unchanged—it was what it was whatever we do or say about it; the second is relative, always changing in response to the increase or refinement of knowledge. The two series correspond more or less; it is our aim to make the correspondence as exact as possible; but the actual series of events exists for us only in terms of the ideal series which we affirm and hold in memory. This is why I am forced to identify history with knowledge of history. For all practical purposes history is, for us and for the time being, what we know it to be. Carl Becker, "Everyman His Own Historian"

The following paragraph defines an idea both by what it is not and by what it is.

Leisure is not idleness, which is neurotic, and still less is it distraction, which is psychotic. Leisure begins in that moment of consciousness peculiar to a rational being, when we become aware

of our own existence and can watch ourselves act, when we have time to think of the worth and purpose of what we are doing, to compare it with what we might or would rather be doing. It is the moment of the birth of human freedom, when we are able to subject what is actual to the standard of what is possible. William Blake calls it the moment in the day that Satan cannot find. It is a terrifying moment for many of us, like the opening of a Last Judgement in the soul, and our highways and television sets are crowded with people who are not seeking leisure but are running away from it. The same is true of the compulsive worker, the man who boasts of how little leisure he has, and who speeds himself up until he explodes in neuroses and stomach ulcers.
Northrop Frye, *University of Toronto Installation Lectures*

8. Analogy: an explanation of one thing in terms of another. The unfamiliar is explained in terms of the familiar. For instance, a computer's ability to retain information may be called its "memory," or socialism may be called a "cancer." The first example uses an analogy between a function of a machine and a function of the human brain in order to explain the nature of the machine. The second example uses an analogy between socialism and a disease in order to express the writer's attitude toward socialism.

Analogy is seldom used as the sole means of organizing a paragraph, but it is often used in conjunction with other methods. In the example below, for instance, the analogy between linguistics and photography provides a dominant frame of reference through three paragraphs (the example quotes only the last sentence of paragraph 2 and all of paragraph 3), but notice that the effectiveness of the analogy is partially dependent upon the use of examples, especially at the end.

. . . If the descriptive linguist takes a photograph of the language, the comparative linguist takes photographs of two or more languages, places the pictures side-by-side, and analyzes their salient features.

The Historical Linguist is easily characterized now: instead of snapshots, he takes movies. His curiosity is directed not at what a language *is* at a given time, but rather at what *made* it what it is. He is a student of development and continuity in language, however, not of the past *per se;* thus he is something of a prophet, something of an amateur visionary: one of his greatest sources of delight is the unfolding of a new linguistic event which allows him a glimpse of the future. For him, the key word in the vocabulary of language study is a simple French loanword: *Change.* A static description of a language at a single moment of time fails to satisfy him, so he puts together a great many "times" (the frames of his movie film strip), and establishes patterns of motion. He may focus his camera on any aspect of language. He may work out the history of sounds or inflections or word meanings. Turning to lexicography he may produce his own kind of dictionary based on historical principles, tracing forms and meanings from the remote past to the present. He may chronicle the rise and fall of a regional dialect, or record the impact of a caravan of wars, invasions, reforms, conversions, and inventions upon a language. In a humbler mood, he may simply write the saga of the comma, or trace the spellings of a word. Louis A. Muinzer, "History: The Life in Language"

9. Classification and division. Paragraphs or groups of paragraphs may be organized by classification of a subject into groups or by division into parts. Sometimes the writer may seem to be merely using a set of numbers to divide his subject into arbitrary categories. But such schemes provide a clear pattern of organization and allow the writer to concentrate on the aspects of the subject which he thinks are most important or most interesting.

It is generally accepted that the tone of a violin is most dependent upon four characteristics of the tone chamber: (1) the type of wood used, (2) the shape and size of the tone chamber, (3) the varnish, and (4) the quality of the workmanship. The purpose of this paper is to explore these characteristics . . . George W. Henry, *Student Theme*

Most Westerns contain three important characters: the hero, the villain, and the heroine.

While attending college, I have had three part-time jobs . . .

Warning: Don't use more divisions than you have time to discuss fully. Each division should be discussed in adequate detail and clearly related to the other divisions.

Pa 3 OPENING AND CLOSING PARAGRAPHS

1. Opening paragraphs. Opening paragraphs should first of all interest the reader in the subject—by the use of an anecdote, an interesting question, a provocative statement, a startling statistic, a quotation, or simply by a clear and cogent exposition of the subject. This last point leads to a second function of opening paragraphs. They usually present a clear statement of the subject, foreshadowing its development and order of presentation in the following paragraphs. Sometimes you may want to use two paragraphs for your introduction, first gaining your readers' interest; then, in a second paragraph, stating the scope and order of presentation of the subject. In writing themes in class, however, you may not have time to develop your introduction as fully as you would like. When writing against time, introduce the subject with directness and economy.

See p. 196.

2. Closing paragraphs. In long papers you may wish to conclude with a summary, but in short papers there is no need for a mechanical and obvious summary of what you have just said. Remember, however, that your last paragraph is the one that leaves a final impression in the reader's mind. Don't weaken that impression with minor details; end strongly on what you consider to be an important point.

See p. 197.

IMPROVING YOUR SKILLS

One indispensable step in learning to write good paragraphs is to become sensitive to them in your reading. When you find a passage that you think is especially good, look carefully at the paragraphs and copy those that you think would make good models for your own writing. After you have collected a number of paragraphs, study them closely (perhaps with the help of your instructor) to determine how they are organized. Then, once you feel that you have understood them, try your hand at using the same patterns, or similar patterns, in a theme of your own. Do this as often as possible until you are able to recognize paragraph patterns and can reproduce them fairly easily. But don't stop there. Keep looking for new patterns and for new ways to use the old ones. Never allow your writing to harden into one or two patterns which you overuse. Some of the basic patterns can be used often without becoming monotonous or distracting, but don't use the same pattern too many times in succession.

As you will notice from your reading and from the examples given above, paragraphs seldom use one method exclusively, although one method is usually dominant. At first you may concentrate on one method at a time, but your goal is to become so proficient in a number of methods that you can select and use an appropriate organizational scheme without conscious effort. Eventually you should be able to concentrate on what you are trying to say and let each paragraph develop as naturally as possible. But remember the four principles in Pa 1. They are pertinent no matter what method you use.

From Beginning to End: The Whole Paper

The two sections that follow cover the whole process of writing a paper, from beginning to end. The first section deals with the decisions and the planning which precede the actual writing of the paper. The second section deals primarily with the process of refining and improving the paper. Between them, they treat the entire process, from choosing and focusing on a topic to the submission of the final revision.

Prewriting

The first step in writing a paper is choosing a topic. Even when the topics are assigned, there is usually some choice among several topics, so your first decision involves choosing the topic which you can write about most effectively. Ideally, it would be a subject about which you have extensive information, which you know about through personal experience, and which you find interesting. Since things are seldom perfect in this world, however, you are not likely to encounter many topics which meet all these criteria. If you have to give priorities, choose on the basis of interest. Even the most interesting topics, however, can be treated in a dull manner, and sometimes what seems to be an unpromising topic can become exciting. A great deal depends on what you do with it.

Once you have selected a topic, there are many ways in which it may be treated. If the topic is a general one, the first step is usually to focus on a specific aspect of the subject which can be treated in the time and space available to you. The subject "Automobiles," for instance, is more appropriate for a book or multivolume encyclopedia than it is for a short paper. The focus would have to be narrowed to a specific but more limited aspect of the subject. One key decision in narrowing the focus is deciding whether you will treat the subject objectively or subjectively. Ask yourself whether you know enough or can learn enough in the time available to write informatively and factually about the subject. If you have adequate information, you might write on a very specific aspect of the subject, such as "The Braking System in the Vega" or "The Wankel Engine," or, somewhat more generally, "Automobile Maintenance" or "Buying a Used Car," or, more generally yet, but still objectively and informatively, "The Future of the Automobile." If, however, you do not have sufficient knowledge to treat the subject impersonally and objectively, you can write about your personal experience with cars. Although you may not know anything about carburetion or the mechanics of the clutch, you certainly know enough about your own personal experience with cars to write about that. You could, for instance, write about an experience such as ''Crossing the Mojave in a Volkswagen'' or you could write on a topic such as ''My First Car,'' or ''The Cars in My Life.'' Another option is to combine the two approaches, drawing upon your store of factual knowledge and combining it with personal experience, in a topic such as ''Working at the Speedway,'' or ''Watching a Pit Stop.''

Different approaches may be implied simply by the way in which you phrase your title: ''Pit Stops'' or ''Deer Hunting,'' for instance, imply different approaches than ''A Pit Stop'' or ''A Deer Hunt.'' The first two topics are likely to be treated impersonally and analytically; the second two are more likely to be based on personal observation or experience.

At any rate, you should be able to find something to write on almost any subject. For instance, consider the topic ''Professional Football.'' A person with a detailed knowledge of the game would be faced with an embarrassment of riches. Since he could not include everything that he knew, his problem would be one of limiting the topic to a manageable scope and deciding what to include and what to leave out. In a short paper of only a few pages, he might decide to write on the contrasting styles of several quarterbacks, or to focus on the characteristics of one coach or one player, or to discuss the responsibilities of the defensive secondary. On the other hand, some persons writing on the topic might not be able to tell a quarterback from a cornerback, and might even find the national mania for football a trifle silly. Such persons would have problems of a different kind, but they too should be able to write about the topic. Anyone who has seen a football game on television has enough material to write on some aspect of the subject if he thinks about it for a while and explores his own attitudes. In fact, since most of us experience football primarily through television, such a person might find television a means of focusing the topic and relating it to his own experience and predilections. He might, for instance, concentrate on the home audience, or discuss the merchandizing of the game on television, or he might speculate as to why football is such a perfect television "event." The factual details would all be there, but the approach would be based on the writer's way of perceiving them.

After deciding whether to treat the subject personally or impersonally and after making an initial reduction in scope, you may have to make further adjustments in the scope of the paper as you go along. For instance, suppose you chose the topic "In the South" and immediately reduced the focus to a narrower and more specific topic, "A Trip to New Orleans." You still would have to decide where to begin, where to end, and what to include in between. If you had only a few pages in which to cover the topic, you would have to decide what aspect of the trip you wanted to stress and come to that part quickly, excluding unnecessary details about other aspects of the trip. For example, one student writing a paper entitled "A Trip to Mardi Gras" decided to include the whole trip, from the morning of his departure to the evening of his return, although the heart of the subject was Mardi Gras in New Orleans. As a result, he spent over half of the paper describing the drive to New Orleans, then had time for only two short paragraphs on Mardi Gras before beginning a hurried effort to make the end of the trip and the end of the paper coincide. Although he thought he had narrowed the focus sufficiently, it was still too broad. He probably should have begun in New Orleans at the height of Mardi Gras. In fact, for a short paper, Mardi Gras itself might be too broad a topic. He probably would have done better yet if he had focused on a particular part of the Mardi Gras festivities that he remembered vividly and that he could have developed in detail.

Personal experiences are relatively easy to write about. Since the experience already has an order of its own imposed by the sequence in which it occurred, you don't have to worry about organizational problems as much as you do in some kinds of writing. But decisions concerning focus and selectivity are still necessary, as they are in every kind of writing.

Once you have focused your topic by establishing the boundaries within which you will be working, you must still decide what to include and what to leave out. It would be a mistake simply to write down everything that comes into your mind. Some details are more important than others, and their importance will vary in accordance with what aspect of the subject you decide to stress. You will need some principle of selection which will give unity to your paper. As an illustration, try the following experiment:

Wherever you are, look around you for a few minutes. Spend, say, two minutes observing as many details as you can—every crack in the ceiling, every chair, every stain on the floor, a shadow on the wall, a belt buckle, shoelaces, a door knob, or whatever details you happen to see.

Now ask yourself how you would use the details that you have observed to write a unified description of the place where you are. You will quickly realize that you could founder amid the abundance of details available to you, even in a small room, unless you find some meaningful order, some principle of selection—whether it be from left to right, from far to near, or simply the degree of prominence of the objects which you see from your position in the room. Many of the details will have to be omitted when they do not fit or when they obscure the pattern which you have chosen. This same principle of selectivity applies to anything that you write. To impose a meaningful order upon the data of experience, you must screen out a great deal of irrelevant material, or, to state the matter positively, you must *select* the material to be included.

At some point in the process of narrowing your focus and

selecting the details which you want to include, you may find it helpful to use the technique called **brainstorming**. This technique uses a period of free association in which you let your mind flow from one thought to another with no effort to control the chain of associations. On a sheet of scratch paper which no one but you will see, jot down at random *any* thought on the topic that comes to mind and let one thing lead to another without worrying about logic or order. Keep this up for five or ten minutes. Remember, anything goes. Keep writing, whether the words seem to make sense or not. The result may seem chaotic at this point, and if you stoppped here it would be, but this is only the first stage.

The next step is to find a pattern for putting things together in a meaningful order. Like the exercise in description above, this is a process of selection and elimination. Again, what you need is a principle of selectivity: a controlling idea or a dominant impression which will provide overall unity in your paper.

Several devices may prove helpful here. As you begin to see a unifying pattern, you can try to state it in a sentence. An attempt to state the idea in a sentence will help you to clarify the pattern of unity that you are seeking. You don't just pull such a sentence out of the air, however. You have to discover it. A controlling idea will evolve as you begin to see relationships between the scattered ideas and details that you have jotted down.

At this stage a scratch outline or a paragraph outline may prove useful.

A **scratch outline** is a rough plan of organization purely for your own convenience. It may consist simply of the central idea of the paper and its main subdivisions, with perhaps a few brief notes on the details to be included and the manner in which the thought is to be developed. Since it is exclusively for your own use while you are working your topic into shape and while you are writing, and since it will be discarded when it is no longer useful, it can take any form that you like—words, phrases, shorthand notations, whatever is most convenient for you. It is a simple, flexible guide with no prescribed form, evolving to fit the flow of your thoughts as you focus your topic, and it is subject to change as you write. It does, however, provide a pattern of order, which allows you to concentrate upon a part of your paper at a time without worrying about what comes next. With its help, you know the scope of your coverage and the order in which you are going to present the subordinate parts of your topic before you begin to write. It provides an overview to which you can refer for guidance at any point in the writing process.

Scratch outlines are especially useful in the early stages of focusing your topic and putting your ideas in order, but they do become messy, and you might want to make use of a paragraph outline or an organizing sentence for the actual writing of the paper. But since *none* of these organizing devices will be seen by the reader, use whatever method works best for you.

A **paragraph outline** can provide a simple but effective guide for a short paper of only a few pages. It consists simply of a thesis statement and a topic sentence for each paragraph to be included in the paper. If you use a paragraph outline, you will know, before you begin to write, the main idea or dominant impression you are trying to develop, the number of paragraphs, the subject of each paragraph, and the order in which the paragraphs are going to be presented.

An **organizing sentence** is even more succinct than a paragraph outline. It simultaneously states the controlling idea and foreshadows the order in which that idea will be developed. The following sentence, for instance, states the controlling idea, presents its subordinate parts, and indicates the order in which they will be discussed:

> Perhaps the main guiding principle of modern architecture is economy: economy of material, economy of means, and economy of expression. Lewis Mumford

This could be an organizing sentence for a short paper of

only three paragraphs, or it could introduce a much longer paper with any number of paragraphs on each of the three subordinate topics. In contrast to outlines, an organizing sentence such as this could actually be included in the paper.

More detailed outlines may be needed as your papers become longer or more complex, but formal outlines such as topic or sentence outlines are primarily for the benefit of the reader, who can use them, much as he would the introduction and table of contents of a book, to gain an overview of the topic and to see the relationship of the parts.

A **topic outline** consists of a thesis statement and a series of divisions and subdivisions of the subject. The major divisions are indicated by roman numerals and are placed on the left margin of the paper. The subdivisions of each major topic are indicated by capital letters (first subdivision), arabic numbers (second subdivision), small letters (third subdivision), and arabic numerals in parenthesis (fourth subdivision). Each subdivision is indented further from the left margin than the topic under which it is placed. All coordinate topics are spaced an equal distance from the margin.

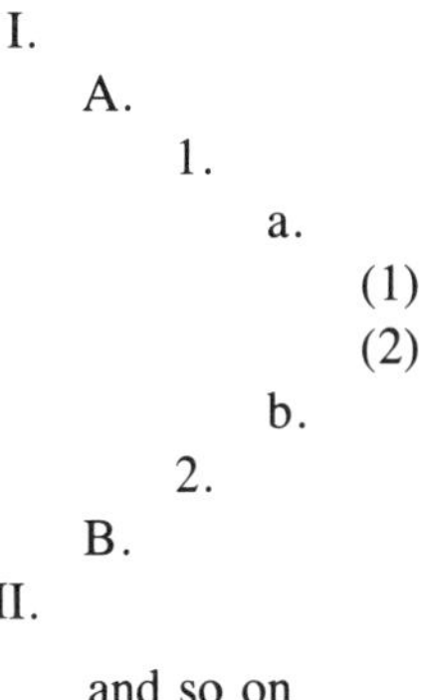

There should be no I without II, no A without B, and so on,

although there is no need to have the same number of subtopics under each heading.

Each heading should be a phrase rather than a complete sentence and should be similar to its coordinate headings in grammatical structure.

The various headings should not overlap each other in the subject matter covered, and the material covered by all of the combined headings should correspond as closely as possible to the idea expressed in the thesis statement.

A **sentence outline** is like a topic outline except that the heading for each division is stated as a complete sentence rather than as a phrase.

Once you have established the scope and the structure of your paper, whatever method you may use, you can concentrate on developing one segment at a time. Simply concentrate as intensely as you can on each section, and try to provide smooth transitions between sections. Some of the methods discussed in Pa 2 (pp. 171ff.) may be useful, but perhaps the main point to remember is to develop each part fully. See Pa 1.3, p. 170.

Revising

There are many kinds of revision. Some of them are minor; others involve major changes. The kind that is used depends upon the type of paper, the amount of time available, and the stage of the paper's development.

Minor changes in word choice and sentence structure may be made as you write. Frequently, sentences or phrases need a little tinkering to make them ring true. Or you may pause to look up the spelling or meaning of a word in your dictionary. The important thing in this kind of revision is not to let it interrupt your main trend of thought. If you do lose your train of thought while working on a troublesome detail, consult your outline to get yourself back on course and, if necessary, quickly read back over the preceding part of your paper to restore your continuity. If you are writing an in-class theme and you are afraid that you won't have time to come back and revise later, then your first draft may have to be the version that you hand in. If so, don't hesitate to cross out and change as you go along. But try to keep your momentum. And don't waste time in recopying your paper. Get your thought down as clearly as you can, and let it stand. If your instructor can read and understand what you have written, it won't matter if it is a little messy—at least not on an in-class paper when you are writing against the clock.

On out-of-class papers, however, you should take full advantage of the opportunity to improve your paper by a comprehensive revision. Literally, revision means re-seeing, or seeing in a new way. But it is very difficult to re-see something you have just written. So when you have time, it is a good idea to put the first version of your paper aside for a while. After the thoughts which you had while writing the paper have cooled, you can see more clearly what you have actually written.

To revise effectively, you need to be a good reader. You have to imagine that you are reading what someone else has written, and yet you have to keep in mind what you, as the writer, were trying to do. It requires that you play a difficult double role, but to rewrite you must first be able to see clearly what you have written and to judge it from the standpoint of a reader.

You need not think of a specific reader, although you could try thinking of a specific reader, or readers, if that helps you to see your writing more objectively. You should not, however, submit completely to the anticipated responses of such a reader, not even if that reader is your instructor. Although you should be respectfully aware of how a reader is likely to respond, you need not simply accept his response as something over which you have no control. You should try to create the response that you would like for him to have. Paradoxically, if you submit too completely to your conception of the reader, you are likely to please neither him nor yourself. You should, instead, indicate by your attitude toward the subject and by the way you phrase your thought how you expect the reader to respond. Hemingway once said that he rewrote the last page of *A Farewell to Arms* thirty-nine times before he was satisfied with it. This is an extreme example. Few writers are so dedicated, and it is quite possible that the thirty-ninth version of an apprentice writer would not be as good as, say, the second or third one. But the point is that Hemingway was not submitting to the response of the reader; he was creating it. He was thinking of the effect he wanted to produce.

While you are revising, you have an opportunity to see your writing in a way that you could not see it while you were in the process of writing it. While you are writing, you necessarily have to concentrate on a part at a time, and it is difficult to constantly see the paper as a whole. (This is one reason for planning the paper before you begin to write.) After you have finished, however, and particularly after you have put your paper aside for a while, it is much easier to examine your work critically and to make thoughtful changes.

Whether you eventually decide to make only minor adjustments or to undertake extensive changes, this is the time to read your paper with an openness toward the possibilities of change. One of the things that you will want to examine carefully is the overall organization of the paper and the relative emphasis upon the parts. You should have done this, of course, in the planning stage before you began to write, but now is the time for second thoughts and for considering ways of improving your original conception. You may want to give some sections relatively more emphasis by adding details or further thoughts, or you may want to eliminate unnecessary or repetitious details. You may decide to add new sections, or to delete old ones, or to shift passages from one spot to another. Large sections of your original version may be dropped from the paper, while others may be expanded or new ones added.

At any rate, your most extensive changes will usually be made after the completion of your first draft—at least on out-of-class papers when there is ample time. On in-class papers you can't hope to get much more than a first draft with a few changes as you go along and a final proofreading for obvious errors. The number of drafts that you write before settling on a final version will depend on the time which you have available and on your evaluation of when you have revised enough. Some people write many drafts, some very few. You will have to discover through practice which combination of forethought, spontaneity, and afterthought works best for you. The result and not the number of revisions is the important thing. A paper *can* be over-revised to the point of becoming tedious. On the other hand, many writers are able, through a series of cumulative revisions, to produce a final version that is immensely superior to their original effort.

Second thoughts on a topic and further, less hurried ideas about how to present it are not always better than your immediate responses, but more often than not they can provide greater depth and more effective ordering to your treatment of the topic.

As your revision reaches its last stages, there are several procedures that can strengthen your paper. First, look back over the paper as a whole, particularly the parts where you have added or deleted passages, to make sure that you have left no rough edges. Read these sections carefully to be sure that the transitions between the parts flow smoothly. You should try to blend the parts so smoothly that the reader will not be aware of where you have made changes.

Then, after the revision has been essentially completed, you should take one more look at the beginning and the ending. Since they create the reader's first and last impressions of the paper, they are the most strategic places in the paper for establishing emphasis, and they should be given special attention. You probably have assumed that the last thing to be written would be the final paragraph, but have you considered writing the beginning last, or at least next to last? There are distinct advantages to writing first things last. For one thing, once everything else has been set, you have a greater awareness of the total paper and you can prepare the reader more fully for what is to come. If you have made changes since writing your first version of the opening paragraph, adjustments should be made so that it is in full accord with what follows. The beginning sets the tone for the whole paper, and therefore it gives you a special opportunity to establish the reader's attitude toward the subject and to guide his responses in the direction in which you want them to go, as well as to give him an overview of the topic. The opening paragraph, then, should be reexamined with the whole paper in mind, and, whenever there is time, it, in conjunction with the concluding paragraph, should receive your final attention.

The conclusion can, of course, be written last. The idea of writing the beginning last is stressed here because the idea might not have occurred to you, but the beginning and the ending should be in harmony, and they should be thought of as complementing each other as you put the finishing touches on your paper. The opening paragraph leads the reader into the subject and prepares him for what follows, and the concluding paragraph offers an opportunity to establish a final unifying emphasis. If you have done a good job in the body of the paper, an explicit summary will not be necessary, but you might want to link the conclusion to the introduction or to an especially important earlier section by echoing a key word or idea which you presented there. Decide what you think is important enough to warrant a final emphasis and stress that, whether it is a final variation on a key idea, a meaningful image, or a climactic action.

Also, let the reader know that the end is near. Don't simply come to an abrupt stop. Sometimes you may want to insert an obvious signal such as "finally," "thus," or "in conclusion," but there are also more subtle ways of letting the reader know that he is nearing the end. One of the most effective ways is to slow the pace of your sentences by the use of parallel constructions, by repetition of key phrases, or simply by longer, more deliberate sentences with internal pauses. The rhythm of your sentences can suggest that you are coming to a conclusion without your having to say so. Above all, take special care to end with a well-phrased sentence that *sounds* like a final sentence. As the reader stops, that sentence will tend to linger in his mind. Try to make it a good one.

You might assume, after a final revision of your opening and closing paragraphs, that you have finished, but a few things remain to be done. The final step before you submit your paper is to edit the entire paper, checking for careless omissions, grammatical errors, punctuation problems, misspelled words, awkward phrasing, and the like. Whether your paper is a short one or a long one, this is an essential step which may produce a marked improvement in the quality of the paper.

One problem in editing is that immediately after you have finished writing you may have difficulty in seeing errors. You may, for instance, look directly at an obvious error and not see it because you see what you are thinking rather than what you have actually written. One way to alleviate this problem is to put your paper aside for a while or, if time is limited, at least to break your train of thought before beginning to proofread. If you are uncertain of the correctness of a particular word or passage, consult your dictionary or the appropriate section in this book (see the inside of the back cover for a quick reference guide).

Another device that will help, particularly after you have written several papers and know the kind of errors that you tend to make, is to make a personal checklist of things to look for while editing. In one of your notebooks, keep a list of the kind of errors you make on each paper, with perhaps a brief summary of your instructor's comments. Gradually this list will reveal to you what you need to be especially alert for in editing. If you know what you are looking for, you can spot problems more easily. Also, by making you more aware of these errors the list may help you to avoid them.

After the final editing, you can submit your paper and forget the rigors of composition for a while, but one step remains. When your paper is returned to you, you will be expected to correct it and to resubmit it for a final check. Your instructor will explain the procedure which he wants you to follow. You almost certainly will be asked to correct all errors, but you may or may not be asked to make major changes.

This final look at your paper is of special importance, for it is at this point that you get feedback from an experienced reader who is trying to help you to improve. Try to read the paper through his eyes and to understand the way he sees it. Every reader will perceive in a slightly different way, but your instructor is trying to serve as an all-purpose reader and to comment in helpful ways upon specific aspects of your writing. You can learn a great deal from understanding what he sees, even if you would not have seen it in quite the same way.

Finally, use this last stage of revision as an opportunity to learn from your mistakes. Any apprentice writer is going to make mistakes; the important thing is how he responds to them when they are pointed out to him. If he tries to ignore them or to justify them, his writing is not going to improve, but if he understands them, he should gradually be able to overcome them. An objective appraisal of the strengths and weaknesses of a paper in the light of your instructor's comments may be the most important step of the whole process of writing and revision. Don't slight it. It can provide insights that lead to improvement on the next paper, or—since there is sometimes a delay in transferring what you have learned to your writing—on the one after that. Revision may be the hardest part of the whole difficult process of learning to write well, but it is through revision that you will learn to improve.

A List of Terms

Absolute phrase. A phrase that contributes to the thought of a sentence but has no grammatical connection to any part of the sentence.

> *His homework completed.* Jim decided to have a beer.
>
> We arrived sooner than we had expected, *the traffic being light.*

Active voice. See *Voice* and G 8, p. 33.

Adjective. A word that modifies a noun or pronoun by describing it more fully or in some way telling more about it. Adjectives are usually placed immediately before nouns or after linking verbs.

> Jane is wearing a *green* dress.
>
> She is *sad.*
> (*Sad* is a predicate adjective modifying *she.*)
>
> Sometimes, but not often in English, adjectives come after nouns.
>
> The streets, *wet* and *gleaming,* reflected the passing headlights.
> (Notice the commas used with adjectives in this position.)

Adverb. A word that modifies a verb, an adjective, or another adverb. An adverb usually comes immediately before the adjective or adverb which it modifies (*extremely* tall, *very* often), but an adverb modifying a verb may be placed either before the verb or after it: "*Immediately* he noticed that something was wrong" or "He noticed *immediately* that something was wrong."

Although a large number of adverbs end in *-ly* (in fact, many adverbs are formed by an *-ly* added to an adjective: *gladly, reluctantly, frequently,* etc.), many adverbs do not end in *-ly* (*seldom, often, almost, never*), and some adjectives end in *-ly* (*friendly, lonely, lovely, slovenly*). Function is more important than form in identifying adverbs. Remember, adverbs modify *verbs, adjectives,* or *adverbs.*

The telephone rang *continually.*

(*Continually* modifies the verb *rang.*)

We watched the *slowly* rising water.

(*Slowly* modifies the participle *rising,* which functions as an adjective.)

She is *extremely* shy.

(*Extremely* modifies the predicate adjective *shy.*)

Mr. Jones speaks *very* rapidly.

(*Very* modifies the adverb *rapidly.*)

Sometimes adverbs are used interrogatively.

Where is he?

When is he coming?

Why did he leave?

Also, adverbs sometimes modify a whole thought or clause rather than just a single word.

Incidentally, we lost the game.

Unpredictably, the jury found him guilty.

Hopefully, the war will end soon.

(Some people object to using *hopefully* in this way, but the construction is becoming increasingly popular.)

See *Conjunctive adverb.*

Analogy. An analogy is a comparison between two (or more) things, implying or stating similarities in such a way that one is used to explain something about the other. See C 4.10 and Pa 2.8.

Antecedent. The antecedent is the word which the pronoun stands in place of.

John is taking *his* car.
(*John* is the antecedent of *his.*)

Mary and *Frank* are taking *their* car.
(*Mary* and *Frank* are the antecedents of *their.*)

Mr. Jones lost *his* hat in a high wind; I saw *him* chasing *it* down the street.
(What is the antecedent of each of the italicized words? *I*, which stands for the speaker, has no written antecedent.)

Antonyms. Words with opposed meanings, as *life, death; implicit, explicit; inductive, deductive.*

Appositive. A word or phrase that refers to the same thing and has the same grammatical construction as a word or phrase which immediately precedes it.

Mr. Jones, our *instructor,* is usually late.
(*Our instructor* is an appositive. It is in apposition with *Mr. Jones.*)

See pp. 50, 52.

Argumentation. Writing that attempts to convince or persuade.

Article. *A, an,* and *the* are articles. They are also function words, since they signal that a noun will follow. See D 10.

Auxiliary verb. An auxiliary verb is a verb added to another verb to form a variation in tense, voice, mood, or emphasis.

AUXILIARIES USED WITH THE VERB *CALL*

Can call, *do* call, *may* call, *will* call, *must* call, *should* call, *would* call, *have* called, *had* called, *am* called, *are* called, *is* called, *have been* called, *shall be* called.

See pp. 23–25.

Case. Case is the name for the system of inflections used to show the function of a noun or a pronoun in a sentence. See G 4.

The nominative case is used for a subject or a predicate noun.

The objective case is used for a direct object, indirect object, object of a preposition, object of a verbal, or subject of an infinitive.

The possessive case, which is formed by adding an apostrophe or an apostrophe and an *s,* is used to indicate ownership (*John's car*) or relationship (*a day's work*).

Clause. A group of words (used as a unit) containing a subject and verb, and sometimes a complement. Independent clauses make sense alone. Dependent clauses, as the name implies, depend upon other clauses for the completion of their meaning. Dependent clauses are further classified according to their use as nouns, adjectives, or adverbs.

INDEPENDENT CLAUSE

Iron rusts.

DEPENDENT CLAUSE

. . . if it rains.

DEPENDENT CLAUSE USED AS A NOUN

I realized immediately *that he was angry.*
(*That he was angry* is used as the direct object of a verb, *realized;* i.e., it is used as a noun.)

DEPENDENT CLAUSE USED AS ADJECTIVE

The man *who is standing by the door* is the coach.
(*Who is standing by the door* is used as an adjective modifying a noun, *man.*)

DEPENDENT CLAUSE USED AS ADVERB

The picnic will be postponed *if it rains*.
(*If it rains* is used as an adverb modifying a verb, *will be postponed.*)

Note: A dependent clause is usually introduced by a subordinate conjunction (*if, because, when, since,* etc.) or by a relative pronoun (*who, which, that*).

For further discussion of clauses, see pp. 47–50.

Collective nouns. Nouns which designate a group thought of as a collective unit: *team, class, committee,* and so on. For subject-verb agreement problems, see G 3.8, p. 8.

Colloquial. Colloquial language is language that is acceptable in conversation or informal writing but not in formal writing.

Complement. A word or group of words that is necessary to complete a grammatical unit. For instance, in the following sentences the words *pretty* (a predicate adjective) and *artist* (a predicate noun) are complements. They are needed to complete the meaning that is partially stated by the subject and the verb.

Jane is *pretty.*

Susan is an *artist.*

Direct objects, indirect objects, and objective complements are also complements.

DIRECT OBJECT

John caught the *ball.*

INDIRECT OBJECT

I gave *him* the book.

OBJECTIVE COMPLEMENT

We elected George *president*.

The italicized words in these three sentences are complements. The meaning would not be complete without them.

Conjugation. The system of inflectional changes (tense, voice, mood, etc.) of a verb. A full conjugation of a verb would list all the inflectional changes possible for that particular verb. See pp. 19–21 for a partial conjugation of the verb *see*.

Conjunction. A word that joins.

Coordinate conjunctions (*and, but, or, nor, for, yet*) join elements of similar grammatical construction (i.e., one independent clause to another, one verb to another, one adjective to another).

Subordinate conjunctions (*as, after, although, because, before, if, while, when, since, than, so that*) introduce dependent clauses and show their relationship to the rest of the sentence.

They have known each other *since* they were children.

He missed the examination *because* he overslept.

They left *before* the game was over.

Note: Some words, like *before*, can be used as more than one part of speech. In the following sentences, for instance, *before* is used as a preposition and as an adverb.

He stood *before* the fire. (preposition)

I have seen this movie *before*. (adverb)

Correlative conjunctions (*either . . . or, neither . . . nor, not only . . . but also*) are conjunctions that are used in pairs. The two parts of a correlative conjunction should be followed by similar (parallel) grammatical units. See S 4, p. 63.

Conjunctive adverb. An adverb that sometimes takes on qualities of a conjunction, especially when placed at the beginning of a clause. For purposes of punctuation, conjunctive adverbs (*then, however, therefore, thus, nevertheless, hence, consequently, moreover, furthermore*) are treated primarily as adverbs. Hence, when a conjunctive adverb is placed between two independent clauses, it is usually preceded by a semicolon or by a period rather than by a comma. (But see Pu 6, p. 129.)

> The temperature was dropping rapidly; *furthermore,* a cold wind was blowing.
>
> (A comma is sometimes placed *after* the conjunctive adverb, but not always. Usually it is optional, depending upon whether or not a pause is desired after the conjunctive adverb.)
>
> The paratrooper hesitated briefly on the threshold; *then* he leaped into space.

Connotation. See D 8, p. 94.

Coordinate conjunction. See *Conjunction.*

Coordination. A coordinate construction is one in which two or more sentence elements (clauses, phrases, nouns, verbs, adjectives, etc.) are given equal importance and similar grammatical construction.

> He came, he saw, he conquered. (coordinate clauses)
>
> Government *of the people, by the people, for the people.* (coordinate phrases)

Our flag is *red, white,* and *blue.* (coordinate adjectives)

Most frequently, however, when one speaks of coordination, he is referring to a combination of independent clauses.

COORDINATION

It began to rain, and *the children ran into the house.*
(Two independent clauses. They are *coordinate.)*

For further comment on coordination, see pp. 48–50.

Correlative conjunction. See *Conjunction.*

Declarative sentences. Sentences that make assertions. They contrast with interrogative sentences, which ask questions.

Declension. A pattern of inflectional changes in a noun or pronoun to show changes in number, case, and (in some pronouns) person. A sample declension of the noun *book* is given below.

	Singular	*Plural*
Nominative case	book	books
Possessive case	book's	books'
Objective case	book	books

Deduction. A method of presenting ideas that proceeds from a general statement to the details or examples that explain, demonstrate, or support the general statement.

Denotation. See D 8, p. 94.

Description. Writing that attempts to depict the physical attributes of an object, scene, or action. In its pure form such writing concentrates on physical characteristics such as size, color, material, sound, feel, smell, or speed; but it is usually mixed with other types of writing such as exposition or narrative.

Dialect. See D 9, p. 95.

Diction. Word choice. The kinds of words that are used and the way in which they are combined.

Direct object. A word or group of words that receives the action of a transitive verb.

> John read the *book*.
> (The noun *book* is the object of the transitive verb, *read.*)
>
> He wanted *me to read the book.*
> (The infinitive phrase, *me to read the book,* is the direct object of the transitive verb, *wanted.*)
>
> John knows *that I like science fiction.*
> (The noun clause, *that I like science fiction,* is the direct object of the transitive verb, *knows.*)

Elliptical clause or sentence. A clause or sentence in which the meaning is not fully stated in words, although it is implied.

> *Although wounded,* the deer escaped.
> (*Although wounded* is an elliptical clause. The full meaning is *Although the deer was wounded,* but only part of the thought is actually stated.)

Expletive. The introductory words in constructions with delayed subjects.

> *There* is a reason for his anger.

Here are my thoughts on censorship.
(The italicized words are expletives.)

Exposition. Writing that attempts to explain or clarify. By far the greatest part of prose writing is expository.

Formal language. Language that is carefully chosen to conform with standard accepted usage. The nature of your audience and the purpose of your writing will determine the degree of formality. A letter of application or recommendation, for instance, will almost always be formal, as will a written report or an address to a large audience. Formal writing avoids any words, phrases, or idioms that might annoy or distract members of the audience.

Function words. Words whose function in relation to other words is more important than their own meaning. Articles, auxiliary verbs, expletives, and prepositions are function words.

Gender. There are four genders in English: masculine (*he, man*), feminine (*she, woman*), neuter (*it, book*), common (*children, student*).

Gerund. A verb form (characteristically ending in *-ing*) used as a noun.

Washing dishes is monotonous.
(*Washing* is a gerund used as the subject of the sentence; i.e., as a noun. Notice that it has a direct object, *dishes.*)

I enjoy *swimming*.
(*Swimming* is a gerund used as the direct object of a verb, *enjoy.*)

He has no time for *studying*.
(*Studying* is a gerund used as the object of a preposition, *for.*)

Grammar. The principles of order which govern a language. The complex of patterns by which words are combined into meaningful statements. The opening section of this book uses the term more restrictively as a label for the most frequent usage problems involving inflectional changes (with pronomial reference included).

Homonyms. Words that sound alike but have different meanings. For example: *site, cite, sight; two, to, too.*

Indirect object. A word that receives the action of a transitive verb indirectly. It is never present unless there is a direct object, and it is placed between the verb and the direct object.

> Mary gave *him* the keys.
> (*Him* is the indirect object of the transitive verb *gave. Keys* is the direct object.)

Induction. A method of presenting ideas that proceeds from particular details and bits of information to a general principle or summary statement.

Infinitive. A verb form (the verb preceded by *to*) used as a noun, adjective, or adverb.

> He likes *to read.*
> (*To read* is an infinitive used as the direct object of the verb *likes;* i.e., used as a noun.)
>
> He is the man *to beat.*
> (*To beat* is an infinitive used as an adjective modifying *man.*)
>
> He came *to see me.*
> (*To see* is an infinitive used as an adverb modifying *came.* It has a direct object, *me.*)

Inflection. A change in the spelling of a word to show a change in its meaning or in its relationship to other words.

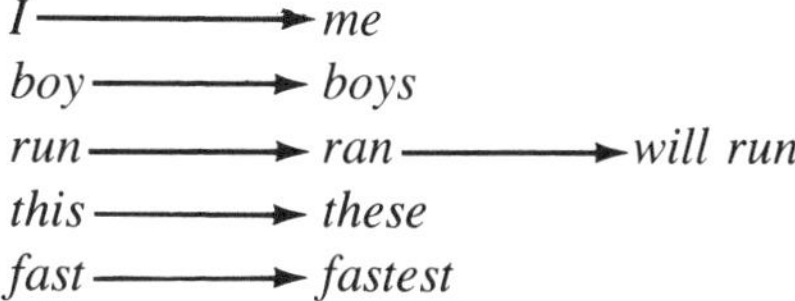

Interjection. A word or phrase that does not affect the basic grammatical construction of the sentence. Usually it provides emphasis.

> *Gosh,* I made an *A* in calculus.
>
> You are going, *aren't you?*
>
> *Yes,* I am going.

Interrogative sentences. Sentences that ask questions.

Intransitive verb. A verb that has no receiver of the action.

> John *smiled.*
> (The action is completed within the verb. No receiver is needed.)

Irony. There are several types of irony, but all are based on contrast. The contrast may be between what is said and what is meant, between what is expected and what actually happens, or between a person's conception of a situation and the reality of the situation. The first type, called *verbal irony,* is by far the most common. After Tybalt has been slain by Romeo, Juliet says to her mother, ''Would none but I might venge my cousin's death.'' Her intended meaning is almost exactly opposite to the meaning which Lady Capulet ascribes to it. Since irony is dependent upon just such a misinterpretation for its characteristic effect, it is particularly treacherous for the unwary reader or listener. Effective irony is based upon deception of at least part of its audience and is appreciated by the alert reader or hearer because of his awareness of the possibilities for misinterpretation. The beginning writer who intends to use irony as a tool should always remember to give his audience some clue to his real meaning; otherwise, his statement will be interpreted literally and he will be completely misunderstood. Yet he must not make his meaning too obvious. The contrast between the literal and implicit meaning may range from complete contradiction (as in Antony's "Brutus is an honorable man") to various shades of qualification.

Linking verb. A linking verb asserts little or no action but serves primarily as a structural link between a subject and a predicate noun or predicate adjective. (See also *Predicate noun, Predicate adjective*.)

> John *is (looks, seems, appears, feels)* nervous.
>
> Harry *is* an artist.
>
> Quinine *tastes (is)* bitter.
>
> The weather *was (turned, became)* cold.

Metaphor. See D 1, p. 87.

Modifiers. Modifiers provide more information about the word they modify, helping the reader to perceive it more clearly and specifically. Modifiers are either adjectives or adverbs, or a group of words used as an adjective or adverb.:

> a *large* house
> (*Large* modifies *house*.)
>
> the *slowly rising* water
> (*Rising* modifies *water; slowly* modifies *rising*.)

the light *in the attic*
(*In the attic* modifies *light.*)

the class *that I like best*
(*That I like best* modifies *class.*)

A, an, and *the* are also modifiers. They are called *articles,* and they are considered to be adjectives; but, rather than giving specific information, they signal the fact that a noun will follow.

Mood. See G 5, p. 14.

Narration. Writing that presents a series of actions arranged in a sequence in time (short story, novel, biography, newspaper report).

Nonrestrictive element. A phrase, clause, or appositive which could be omitted without changing the basic meaning of the sentence. Nonrestrictive elements are separated from the rest of the sentence by commas.

I was astonished to learn that Jones, *whom I had seen only a few hours before,* was dead.
(The dependent clause *whom I had seen only a few hours before* is nonrestrictive and is therefore separated from the rest of the sentence by commas.)

The principle stated above is not applied rigorously to prepositional phrases. The current tendency is not to separate prepositional phrases from the rest of the sentence by commas unless they are long phrases placed at the beginning of the sentence or unless the writer wants a distinct pause before and after them.

Noun. A word that can be used in the following ways:

Subject of a verb: *John* smiled.

Predicate noun: Henry is an *athlete*.

Subject of an infinitive: She wanted *John* to go.

Direct object of a verb: Mr. Patterson likes *television*.

Indirect object of a verb: She baked *John* a cake.

Object of a preposition: To see yourself on *television* is a strange experience.

Object of an infinitive: We wanted to see the *game*.

Appositive: He was reading his favorite author, *Hemingway*.

Sometimes a phrase or clause may be used as a noun.

To see yourself on television is a strange experience.
(The whole infinitive phrase *to see yourself on television* is used as the subject of *is*.)

I knew *that he was angry*.
(The entire clause *that he was angry* is used as the direct object of *knew*.)

Washing dishes is monotonous.
(The gerund phrase *washing dishes* is used as the subject of *is*.)

A noun may also be called a *substantive*, an alternate and more general term. Since all of the italicized words or groups of words in this section are used as nouns, they are also substantives.

The same word may be used as a noun or as some other part of speech. *Murder*, for instance, is frequently used as a noun, but consider the sentence "Macbeth *murdered* Duncan." In this case both the position (between two nouns) and the inflectional ending *-ed* indicate that the word is being used as a verb. On the other hand, consider the sentence "I once witnessed a *murder*." Here you know that *murder* is a noun because it is used as the direct object of the verb *witnessed* (and also because it is preceded by the article *a*).

Number. Number indicates whether a word is singular or plural. Both nouns and verbs change their spelling to show number; but, except in the verb *to be* (*am, are, is,* etc.), verbs change only in the third person singular in the present and present perfect tenses.

I *walk,* you *walk,* but he *walks*

I *have* walked, you *have* walked, but he *has* walked

Most English nouns are changed from singular to plural by adding *-s* or *-es*.

boy ⟶ boys
fox ⟶ foxes

For exceptions (such as *child, children* or *phenomenon, phenomena*) learn how to find the plural form of words in your dictionary.

Objective complement. An adjective or noun that follows the direct object and further explains or qualifies it.

We painted the house *white*.

We elected George *president*.

Organizing sentence. A sentence that states the subject of a paper and foreshadows the order in which it will be developed.

Radio has at least three advantages over television: it offers more variety, a wider range of use, and fewer commercials. (This sentence indicates the basic organization of the paper. The sub-topics would be discussed in the order in which they are named.)

See p. 190.

Participle. A verb form used as an adjective. It characteristically ends in *-ed, -en, -t* (past participle) or in *-ing* (present participle).

We watched the *surging* tide.
(*Surging* is a present participle modifying a noun, *tide.*)

The wind whistled through the *broken* window.
(*Broken* is a past participle modifying a noun, *window.*)

Passive voice. See *Voice* and G 8, p. 33.

Person. Perhaps the best way to explain the meaning of *person* is to give examples. *Person* is illustrated below by the so-called "personal " pronouns (in the nominative case).

	Singular	*Plural*
First person	I	We
Second person	You	You
Third person	He, she, it	They

Phrase. A group of words which does not contain a verb and which is used as a unit. Phrases may be classified in two ways: (1) according to key words—preposition, participle, gerund, infinitive; (2) according to use—noun, adjective, adverb.

He walked *to the car.*
(*To the car* is a prepositional phrase used as an adverb modifying *walked.*)

The girl *in the red dress* is Mary.
(*In the red dress* is a prepositional phrase used as an adjective modifying *girl.*)

He watched the waves *breaking on the shore.*
(*Breaking on the shore* is a participial phrase used as an adjective modifying the noun *waves.*)

He enjoys *reading poetry.*
(*Reading poetry* is a gerund phrase used as the direct object of a verb, *enjoys. Poetry* is a direct object of a gerund, *reading.*)

He asked *me to go.*
(*Me to go* is an infinitive phrase used as a noun; it is the direct object of *asked.*)

He came *to see me.*
(*To see me* is an infinitive phrase used as an adverb modifying *came.*)

He has much work *to do.*
(*To do* is an infinitive phrase used as an adjective modifying *work.*)

Predicate. In its broadest sense, that which is asserted about the subject in a sentence, including the verb and all of its complements and modifiers. The verb is the key word in the predicate, and sometimes the verb alone is called the predicate.

Snow *changes the familiar landscape into a world of surprising surfaces and shadows.*
(All of the sentence except the word *snow* is the predicate. *Snow* is the subject.)

Predicate adjective. An adjective following a linking verb (*am, is, are, become, seem*) and modifying the subject of the verb.

The wind is *cold.*

Predicate noun. A noun (or pronoun) following a linking verb (*am, is, are, become*) and modifying the subject of the verb.

George is a *poet.*
(*Poet* is a predicate noun.)

Preposition. A word used to indicate the relationship of a following noun or pronoun to the rest of the sentence. Typical prepositions are *in, into, of, beyond, over, under, between, across, behind, to, for.*

He fell *down* the stairs.
(*Down* links the noun *stairs* to the rest of the sentence and shows its relationship to the rest of the sentence.)

Progressive forms. Verb forms that indicate a continuing action. Progressive verb forms end in *-ing* and are preceded by some inflection of the verb *be*. The progressive form can be used in any tense.

PRESENT

He *is shutting* the door.

PAST

He *was shutting* the door.

FUTURE

He *will be shutting* the door all day.

The progressive form can also be used in the passive voice.

The door *is being shut.*

Pronoun. A word that may be substituted for a noun or another pronoun. The word for which the pronoun is substituted is called its *antecedent*. Pronouns are classified as follows:

PERSONAL PRONOUNS

I, you, he, she, it, we, they

RELATIVE PRONOUNS

who, which, that

INTERROGATIVE PRONOUNS

who, which, what

INDEFINITE PRONOUNS

some, any, one, each, few, all, someone, anybody, everybody

DEMONSTRATIVE PRONOUNS

this, that, these, those

INTENSIVE PRONOUNS

myself, yourself, himself, herself, itself, ourselves, themselves

REFLEXIVE PRONOUNS

The same as intensive pronouns

Intensive and reflexive pronouns are distinguished from each other by their use. Intensive pronouns merely serve for emphasis and do not affect the grammatical structure of the clauses in which they appear. Reflexive pronouns serve as an essential part of the grammatical structure of the clauses in which they appear.

INTENSIVE

I will do it *myself.*

REFLEXIVE

I hurt *myself.*
(*Myself* is the direct object of a verb, *hurt.*)

Indefinite pronouns are especially troublesome in the matter of agreement. See G 2, p. 4.

Redundance. An unnecessary repetition of meaning.

The house was white *in color.*

(The phrase *in color* is redundant and should be deleted from the sentence.)

Restrictive element. A phrase, clause, or appositive which cannot be omitted from the sentence without changing the basic meaning of the sentence or omitting essential details. Restrictive elements are not separated from the rest of the sentence by commas.

Men *who drive recklessly* are fools.
(The dependent clause, *who drive recklessly,* is restrictive and therefore is not separated from the rest of the sentence by commas.)

Standard English. The usage that is most widely accepted as correct by discriminating writers and speakers.

Subject. The part of the sentence about which something is said in the predicate.

Mary likes John.
(*Mary* is the subject.)

She likes John.
(*She* is the subject.)

Driving on ice is hazardous.
(*Driving on ice* is the subject.)

To be objective about one's self is difficult.
(*To be objective about one's self* is the subject.)

What happened next was a complete surprise.
(*What happened next* is the subject.)

Nouns, pronouns, gerund phrases, infinitive phrases, or some dependent clauses may be used as subjects.

Subordinate Conjunction. See *Conjunction.*

Subordination. Phrasing one part of a sentence so that it is grammatically dependent on another. Often you have the choice of making a part of a sentence either coordinate or subordinate. If one part of a sentence is coordinate to another part, it is equal to that part in structure. If it is subordinate to the other part, it is dependent upon the other part for the completion of its meaning.

COORDINATE

The wind began to blow, and *the fire spread quickly.*
(The two clauses are given equal weight. They are coordinate.)

SUBORDINATE

As the wind began to blow, the fire spread quickly.
(The first clause is dependent upon the second clause for the completion of its meaning. It is *subordinate* to the second clause.)

See S 5, p. 64.

Substantive. A word or group of words used as a noun. See *Noun.*

Synonyms. Words whose meanings are very nearly the same, with only slight shades of difference. For example: *critical, crucial; insipid, vapid, banal; concise, terse, succinct.*

Syntax. The principle of arrangement by which the words of a sentence are related to each other in a meaningful order. In the following sentence, for instance, the syntactical pattern is that of *subject-verb-object.*

John hit the ball.

But the pattern is exactly the same in this sentence.

The ball hit John.

We know immediately which word is the subject in each case because of our experience with English syntax. The order of the words indicates their relationship to each other.

Tense. In the conjugation of a verb, the tense system indicates the time at which the action takes place (in relation to the time of writing or speaking).

There are six tenses in English (indicated below by the first person singular active indicative of each tense, with the progressive forms in parenthesis).

PRESENT

I think (am thinking)

PAST

I thought (was thinking)

FUTURE

I shall think (shall be thinking)

PRESENT PERFECT

I have thought (have been thinking)

PAST PERFECT

I had thought (had been thinking)

FUTURE PERFECT

I shall have thought (shall have been thinking)

A full discussion of tense can be found in G 7, p. 18.

Theme. A theme is a short writing exercise which develops one basic idea or one dominant impression fully and clearly.

Thesis statement. A statement, in one or two sentences, of the central idea of a paper or outline.

Tone. The author's attitude toward his subject and toward his audience as it is revealed in specific words and phrases, but particularly in the *connotations* of what he says. The tone may be humorous, ironic, serious, angry, urgent, and so on.

Topic sentence. A sentence which explicitly states the central thought of the paragraph in which it occurs. Usually it is the first sentence in the paragraph, although it may come elsewhere. Not all paragraphs have topic sentences. See Pa 1.1, p. 169, and Pa 2.3, pp. 174–175.

Transitive verb. A verb that has a receiver of the action.

> John *polished* the car.
> (*Car,* the direct object, receives the action asserted by the verb, *polished.* The verb is transitive—active voice.)
>
> The car *was polished* by John.
> (*Car,* the subject, receives the action asserted by the verb, *was polished.* The verb is transitive—passive voice.)

Verb. The key word in an assertion. In the following sentences the verbs are italicized.

> Snow *fell* all night.
>
> Snow *has fallen* all night.
>
> Snow *lies* in deep drifts against the door.
>
> Snow *is* beautiful, but it *can be* dangerous.

Notice that the important thing about a verb is how it functions. For instance, the word *love* is a noun in the first sentence below, but a verb in the second one.

> *Love* is a mystery.
>
> I *love* my wife.

Verbs are characterized by auxiliaries and inflectional endings such as *-ed* or *-en (has burned, could have broken)* and by *-s* in the third person singular of the present tense (he *loves*).

See *Sentence Structure*, pp. 38–43. Also see *Voice, Mood, Tense, Connugation*.

Note: Do not confuse *verbs* with *verbals*.

Verbal. A verb form which, though still retaining some characteristics of a verb (i.e., sometimes having a subject or a direct object), functions as a noun, adjective, or adverb. There are three kinds of verbals: gerunds, participles, and infinitives.

Voice. The voice of a verb is either active or passive. If the subject performs the action of the verb or is the subject of a linking verb, the verb is said to be in the *active voice*. If the subject receives the action of the verb, the verb is said to be in the *passive voice*.

ACTIVE VOICE

John *polished* the car.

John *is* proud of his car.

PASSIVE VOICE

The car *was polished* by John.

See G 8, p. 33.

Theme Topics

These topics are intended to help the student discover experiences or ideas that he can write about. Each person must find his own meaning and order in them.

The topics are numbered so that the teacher can on occasion arbitrarily assign certain numbers for a particular writing assignment. He can also, of course, carefully select certain topics, or he can give the students a free choice. The lists may also prove useful as a stimulus for inventing new topics.

Incidentally, these topics can also be used for practice sentences and paragraphs, and some of them may be used successfully more than once.

1. A Careful Choice
2. Scars
3. A Ritual
4. My Father's World
5. Parallels
6. Moving Out
7. Violence
8. In the Fields
9. His Books (or Book)
10. A Festival
11. A Darkened Room
12. Justice
13. Inches
14. Crocodile Tears
15. Polluted
16. A Salesman
17. On the Ice
18. An Artist
19. An Unexpected Answer
20. Heroines
21. A Classroom Scene
22. A Service Station
23. An Incident in the Supermarket
24. Christ Now
25. Harvest
26. The New ——— (House, Car, Job, etc.)
27. The Old ——— (Man, School, Car, etc.)
28. Signs
29. First Prize
30. Music to My Ears
31. Falling
32. Fallen
33. The Mistake

34. Ripe
35. Laughter
36. Escape
37. Precision
38. Full
39. Idols and Idolatry
40. Efficiency
41. A Family Custom
42. An Object As Symbol
43. Fear
44. Smoke
45. Running
46. Buying ———
47. Selling ———
48. Waiting
49. Listening
50. Commuting
51. Lost
52. Found
53. Alone
54. Faces
55. A Dream
56. A Teacher
57. Revival
58. A Race
59. A Failure
60. Sounds
61. A Hero
62. Grades
63. Children
64. Praying
65. A Specialist
66. The Enemy
67. Faith
68. Facts
69. Masks
70. Lost and Found
71. Then and Now
72. Speaker and Audience
73. Television Commercials
74. Radio Commercials
75. Radio and Television
76. Men and Machines
77. A Simple Pleasure
78. An Act of Courage
79. An Act of Kindness
80. Night Journey
81. A Price Tag
82. An End and a Beginning
83. Broken Glass
84. No Man Is an Island
85. Where Are They?
86. A Problem of Communication
87. Success As Failure
88. A Cold Wind Was Blowing
89. I Disagree
90. You Shall Know Them by Their Fruits
91. The Turning Point
92. The Anatomy of a Job
93. The Highway
94. On the Road
95. Automobiles
96. Building a ———
97. Repairing a ———
98. Flowing Water
99. The Trip
100. Old Men
101. Teamwork
102. A Hidden Prejudice
103. Holiday—Holy Day
104. Losing His (or Her) Cool
105. Other Worlds

106. Another World
107. Behind Bars
108. A Badge
109. Manic
110. Coach (or Coaches)
111. A New Perspective
112. Two ——— (Teachers, Cars, Merchants, etc.)
113. Free
114. The Last Inch
115. Mad As a March Hare
116. Children and Fools Cannot Lie
117. Promises
118. Time Clarifies
119. A Stranger in a Strange Land
120. Blind Guides
121. The Letter Killeth
122. First Impressions
123. Installing a ———
124. Fishing for ———
125. Training for ———
126. Arrivals and Departures
127. Motels
128. Getting Ready
129. Hair
130. A Trial Run
131. Practice
132. At the Races
133. An Interview
134. A Witness
135. Shoes
136. In the Wilderness
137. On the Mountain
138. Fast
139. Walls
140. A Bridge
141. Exploring ———
142. The Assembly Line
143. In the Ghetto
144. A Suburban ——— (Day, Home, Scene, Crisis, etc.)
145. A Season in Hell
146. Clubs
147. The Boss
148. Boys and Men
149. Slinging Slang
150. Girls and Women
151. A Victim
152. Antiques
153. Mill Life
154. A Commune
155. A Farmer's Tale
156. The Bill
157. Moonlighting
158. Crossing the Desert
159. A Useful Tool
160. A Woman's Place
161. Playing the Market
162. Door to Door
163. Poverty
164. Affluence
165. The Editorial Page
166. Cameras
167. Behind the Camera
168. Delivering
169. Weekly
170. On the Trail
171. Old Cowboys
172. Under Water
173. Indians
174. Beach Life
175. The Celluloid World

176. City Streets
177. Parks
178. The Image Makers
179. Dates
180. In the Museum
181. Behind the News
182. Fashions
183. While It Lasts
184. A Nice Profit
185. The Loss of Privacy
186. The Craftsman
187. Artists
188. Trapped
189. House As Status
190. House As Home
191. Therapy
192. The National Pastime
193. Uncle ———
194. Outside the Church
195. Finding a Scapegoat
196. Heroes and Villains
197. Words and Deeds
198. The Monster
199. The New House
200. The New House Ages
201. The Old Church
202. The New Church
203. A Real Bargain
204. Campaigning
205. Junk City
206. Body Language
207. Tracks
208. Anatomy of a Machine
209. How It Works
210. The Making of a Path
211. Earth and Asphalt
212. The Four Corners
213. Traffic
214. ——— [supply a number] Seconds
215. Addicts
216. Hypocrisy
217. Night Life
218. Noise
219. A Quiet Place
220. Silence
221. Rock
222. How Many Highways?
223. The Finished Product
224. Unfinished Business
225. All the Moves
226. A Beauty Contest (or Beauty Contests)
227. The Wilderness near Boston (or any other city)
228. Neon Art
229. Hard Work
230. Moving
231. Up There
232. The Last Time
233. A Dying Art
234. A World of Wheels
235. The Graveyard
236. A Country Store
237. Kitchen Life
238. Home
239. In Winter
240. An Identity Crisis
241. Children's Games
242. Leaving the City
243. Power Corrupts
244. The Rites of Ignorance
245. The End of Innocence
246. A Low Ceiling

247. A Wilderness of Signs
248. A Place: Day and Night
249. A Place: Crowded and Empty
250. Pushing
251. A Broken Promise
252. A Lost Chance
253. Bones
254. The Automobile Graveyard
255. Rush Hour
256. Styles of Leisure
257. Mass Production
258. In the Bank
259. Winning and Losing
260. A Winner Who Lost
261. Another Chance
262. A Hobby
263. Closed Doors
264. A Broken Toy
265. Bottles, Cans, and Sacks
266. An Accident
267. Guns
268. Why I Am Here
269. Dieting
270. A Habit
271. On the River
272. A Long Way
273. The Neon Jungle
274. The Answer
275. A Lost Joy
276. A Mirror (or Mirrors)
277. On the Stage
278. A Person Who Changed My Life
279. An Experience that Changed My Life
280. Houses of the Rich
281. Two Doors
282. A Broken Record
283. The Key (or Keys)
284. The Bench
285. Gone
286. Skin
287. A Successful Party
288. Down There
289. Up and Down
290. Why I Laughed
291. Houses of the Poor
292. Landmarks
293. Labels
294. Playing with Dolls
295. A Family Crisis
296. The World of Charley Brown
297. Without TV
298. Foreign Cars
299. An Unusual Sport
300. A Discovery
301. Faces in the Crowd
302. A Change of Mind
303. Five Hundred Miles (substitute any number) from My Home
304. Clothes in Winter
305. An Old Photograph (use or think of an actual photograph)
306. Hitting Bottom
307. The Wall
308. Skiing
309. Another Season
310. Seldom Seen
311. Little Rituals
312. This Room

313. Hardware
314. Teeth
315. A Layer of Dust
316. A Survivor
317. Flying
318. American Pastoral
319. On the Land
320. Planting
321. Whitewater
322. The Water's Edge
323. Old Farm, New Farmer
324. Hidden Costs
325. Fatigue
326. Winterscape
327. A Costly Error
328. The Next War
329. A Summer Job
330. Fishermen
331. Blood
332. Only a Game
333. My Turn
334. The Fifth Season
335. Hunters
336. Barter
337. Traps
338. Changing Styles
339. A Wheelchair
340. Job Hunting
341. The Big Trucks
342. Empty
343. Hardhats
344. The Arrival of the Bulldozer
345. Superstars: A Comparison
346. Blue Collar Blues
347. Money for Sale
348. A Car for Sale
349. An Unexpected Joy
350. Travelers
351. An Investment
352. Night Work
353. The Flood
354. Burnt
355. The Band (or Bands)
356. Beneath
357. A Delicate Balance
358. Stolen
359. Ah, Mexico
360. Farm Life
361. Janus (see your dictionary)
362. The Short Way
363. Monuments
364. Street Life
365. Old Athletes
366. A Broken Chain
367. Hands (supply an adjective: quick, soft, dirty?)
368. Windows
369. Black Athletes
370. Cowboys
371. Shoplifting (or Shoplifters)
372. Television Sports
373. Cycles
374. The Long Haul
375. Headlights
376. Fish
377. Solar Energy
378. Night Changes
379. Blue Collars and White
380. Breaking the Habit
381. A Misunderstanding
382. Two Pictures
383. A Restoration
384. Gone

385. A House on Wheels
386. Where It Stood
387. A Clown
388. Television Sounds
389. An Imaginary Conversation
390. Row after Row
391. Television Images
392. Seeds
393. Amazing Grace
394. Graffiti
395. Taken for Granted
396. Dylan
397. Concerts (or A Concert)
398. His (or Her) Way
399. The Inland Sea
400. An Old Song
401. Country Music
402. Names on the Land (look at a map, if possible)
403. Closed
404. First Things Second
405. The Wind Blows Free
406. Women Athletes
407. Kinfolks
408. House Styles
409. Keeping Warm
410. Boats
411. Question and Answer
412. Cross-Purposes
413. Where the Road Forks
414. Coping with Computers
415. On the Market
416. Speed
417. In the Middle
418. Jokes
419. Profit Margins
420. Junk
421. Divorce As a Way of Life
422. The Answer Is Yes (or No)
423. The Rodeo
424. A Letter to the Editor
425. Sales Craft
426. River Traffic
427. Westward
428. Trading
429. Baptist Styles
430. New Clothes
431. Our Shakespeare
432. Safe
433. What's in a Name?
434. Brand Names
435. Lies
436. Sins of Omission
437. Behind the Scenes
438. The New Cars
439. Network News
440. True or False
441. A Gift
442. A Visit to the Hospital
443. Life and Death
444. The Marijuana Farm
445. A Kind of Trophy
446. Nashville
447. A Little Ball
448. Defense
449. Plagiarism
450. A Dull Party
451. Prisons (or A Prison)
452. Prisoners
453. A Musician (or Group)
454. Competition
455. Horses
456. A Carpenter

457. Bricks
458. Trial and Error
459. A Killing Frost
460. The Barn
461. Racing
462. Ennui (see your dictionary)
463. Crafts
464. Rock Fans
465. Watching It Happen
466. A Rodeo Event
467. Northward
468. Stock Cars
469. Beyond Defeat
470. O Pioneers
471. The Pipeline
472. A World of Machines
473. A Plastic World
474. A Beautiful Girl
475. Radio Stations
476. Punching Buttons
477. Back Roads
478. The Road Back
479. Plains, Georgia
480. Terra Incognita (see your dictionary)
481. The First Stone
482. One Dollar
483. Sitting There
484. Las Vegas
485. Dark Amidst the Blaze of Noon
486. Golf in Winter
487. Wrestling
488. Quarterbacks
489. Customers
490. A Scene (or Scenes) from a Movie
491. Homage to a Loser
492. Human Error
493. Along the Coast
494. Mindless Perfection
495. Through Indian Eyes
496. Collecting (or Collectors)
497. Lost in the Supermarket
498. The Black Market
499. A ——— Hunt (fill in the blank: deer, fox, man?)
500. Dictionary Roulette (Open your dictionary at random and put your finger on the page. The word your finger points to is your topic. If the first choice doesn't seem promising, try again.)

Index

Key to Abbreviations and Symbols

Ab	Abbreviation	M 1	(p. 145)
Adj	Adjective Form	G 1	(p. 1)
Adv	Adverb Form	G 1	(p. 1)
Amb *or* ?	Ambiguous	C 1	(p. 78)
Apos	Apostrophe	Pu 1	(p. 121)
Awk	Awkward Construction	S 7	(p. 68)
Bib	Bibliography	M 4	(p. 158)
Brak	Brackets	Pu 2	(p. 121)
Cap	Capitalization	Pu 19, M 2	(pp. 140, 145)
Case	Case	G 4	(p. 10)
CEC	Confusing Elliptical Clause	S 10	(p. 71)
Cliché	Cliché	D 3	(p. 89)
Comp	Comparison	C 2	(p. 79)
Con	Connotation	D 8	(p. 94)
Cord	Coordination	S 5	(p. 64)
CS	Comma Splice	Pu 6	(p. 128)
DD	Distracting Details	C 3	(p. 79)
DM	Dangling Modifier	S 2	(p. 60)
Doc	Documentation	M 3	(p. 147)
D-W	Deadwood	D 4	(p. 90)
FP	False Predicate	S 16	(p. 76)
Frag	Fragment	S 1	(p. 59)
FS	False Subject	S 16	(p. 76)
Fus	Fused Sentence	Pu 10	(p. 132)
GAD	Generalized or Abstract Diction	D 5	(p. 91)
Hyp	Hyphen	Pu 11	(p. 133)
Id	Idiomatic Usage	D 6	(p. 92)
Inv	Inversion	S 11	(p. 72)
Ital	Italics	Pu 12	(p. 134)
Jar	Jargon	D 7	(p. 93)
K	Awkward Construction	S 7	(p. 68)
K Shift	Awkward Shift	S 9	(p. 70)
Logic?	Questionable Logic	C 4	(p. 80)
LQt	Long Quotation	Pu 20	(p. 140)
Mx	Mixed Construction	S 8	(p. 69)
MM	Misplaced Modifier	S 3	(p. 61)
MMt	Mixed Metaphor	D 1	(p. 87)